PUFFIN BOOKS

JOURNEYS OF EMPIRE

Also by Sathnam Sanghera

STOLEN HISTORY

JOURNEYS OF EMPIRE

BRITISH VOYAGES THAT CHANGED THE WORLD FOREVER – AND THE REBELS WHO RESISTED

SATHNAM SANGHERA

Illustrated by Jen Khatun

PUFFIN

PUFFIN BOOKS

UK | USA | Canada | Ireland | Australia
India | New Zealand | South Africa

Puffin Books is part of the Penguin Random House group of companies whose addresses can be found at global.penguinrandomhouse.com.

www.penguin.co.uk   www.puffin.co.uk   www.ladybird.co.uk

First published 2025

001

Text copyright © Sathnam Sanghera, 2025
Illustrations copyright © Jen Khatun, 2025

The moral right of the author and illustrator has been asserted

The brands mentioned in this book are trademarks belonging to third parties

The map on pages vi–vii includes data from Dimitrios licensed from AdobeStock (under licence number 565858264).

The diagram on page 48 includes data from Archivist licensed from AdobeStock (under licence number 162386071).

The illustration on page 158 includes material from Archivist licensed from AdobeStock (under licence number 247743419).

Penguin Random House values and supports copyright. Copyright fuels creativity, encourages diverse voices, promotes freedom of expression and supports a vibrant culture. Thank you for purchasing an authorized edition of this book and for respecting intellectual property laws by not reproducing, scanning or distributing any part of it by any means without permission. You are supporting authors and enabling Penguin Random House to continue to publish books for everyone. No part of this book may be used or reproduced in any manner for the purpose of training artificial intelligence technologies or systems. In accordance with Article 4(3) of the DSM Directive 2019/790, Penguin Random House expressly reserves this work from the text and data mining exception.

Set in 10.5/17pt Sabon LT Std
Typeset by Six Red Marbles UK, Thetford, Norfolk
Printed and bound in Great Britain by Clays Ltd, Elcograf S.p.A.

The authorized representative in the EEA is Penguin Random House Ireland, Morrison Chambers, 32 Nassau Street, Dublin D02 YH68

A CIP catalogue record for this book is available from the British Library

ISBN: 978–0–241–74141–2

All correspondence to:
Puffin Books, Penguin Random House Children's
One Embassy Gardens, 8 Viaduct Gardens, London SW11 7BW

Penguin Random House is committed to a sustainable future for our business, our readers and our planet. This book is made from Forest Stewardship Council® certified paper.

*My thanks to Jessica Bullock,
Sarah Chalfant, Phoebe Jascourt,
Alan Lester, Lottie Moggach,
Catherine Phipps, Michael Taylor
and Kate Teltscher.*

A MAP OF THE WORLD, 1923

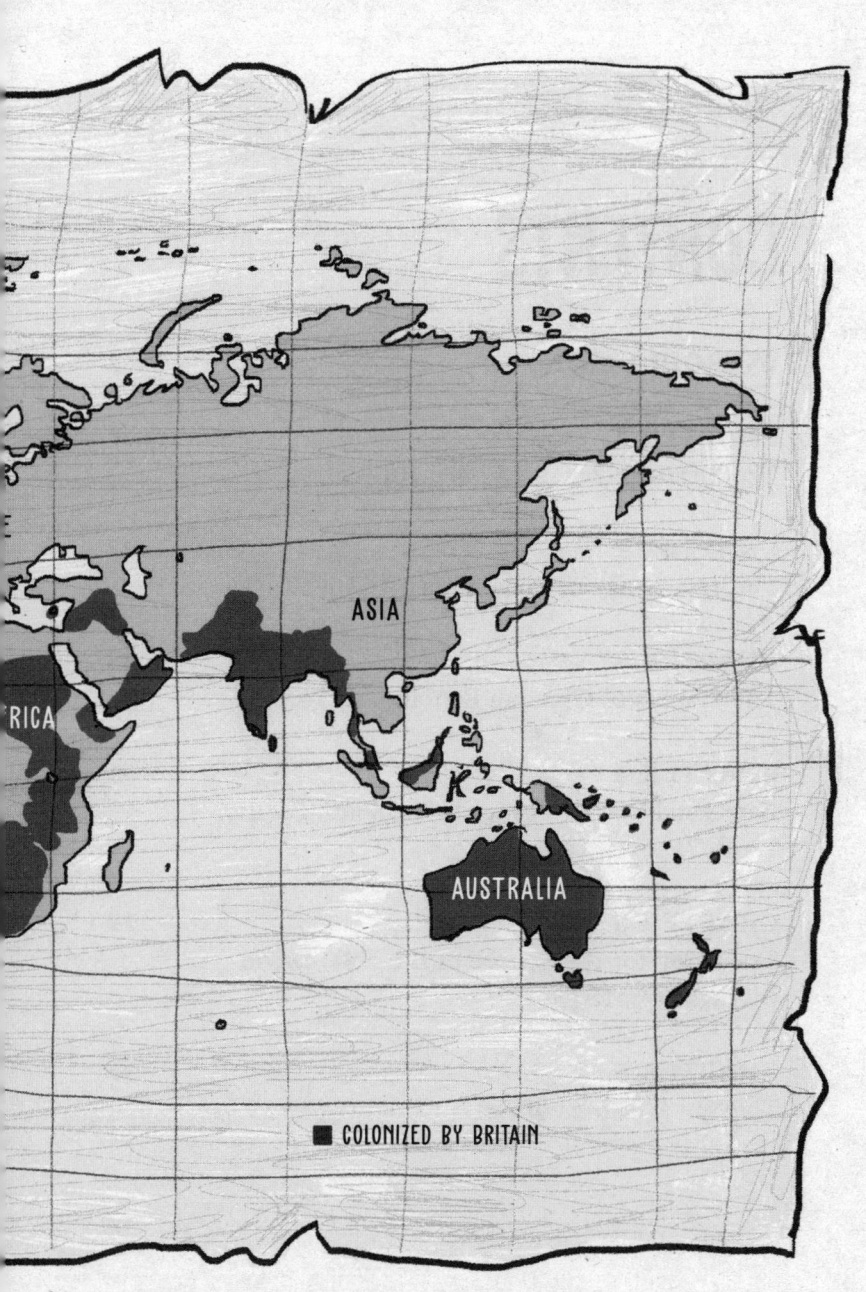

CONTENTS

INTRODUCTION — 1

CHAPTER 1 — 9
The Pirate Queen, c.1530–c.1603

CHAPTER 2 — 27
The True Story of Pocahontas, 1616–17

CHAPTER 3 — 45
The Travels of Olaudah Equiano, c.1745–97

CHAPTER 4 — 61
Banks and Cook's Voyage to the South Pacific, 1768–71

CHAPTER 5 — 79
Searching for the Source of the Nile: David Livingstone, 1813–73

CHAPTER 6 — 97
The Spy Missions of Arthur Conolly, 1829–41

CHAPTER 7 113
The Voyage of *Hesperus* and *Whitby*, 1838

CHAPTER 8 129
Adventures in the Middle East: Gertrude Bell, 1868–1926

CHAPTER 9 147
The Younghusband Expedition to Tibet, 1903–04

CHAPTER 10 163
A Luxurious Trip to India, 1911–12

CHAPTER 11 181
Gandhi and the Salt March, 1930

CONCLUSION 197

QUESTIONS AND CONVERSATIONS ABOUT THE BRITISH EMPIRE 201

INDEX 204

INTRODUCTION

INTRODUCTION

Think of something really, really big, and I bet that the British Empire was bigger. Russia? Not a bad place to start: it's the largest country in the modern world. It covers a staggering 6.3 million square miles and about eleven per cent of the world's land surface. But no, it isn't bigger than the British Empire was. The British Empire covered nearly 14 million square miles, or a quarter of the planet's land surface, at its height in 1923 – this is more than twice the area that Russia covers today.

What about Pluto? I assume you mean the dwarf planet rather than the cartoon dog? Funny you should suggest it, because Pluto's surface area is roughly the same size as Russia. So again, the British Empire, when it reached its height, on Saturday 29 September 1923, was more than twice as big as this entire dwarf planet.

The moon? OK, you might have got me there. But only just. The surface area of the moon is about 14.6 million square miles, which is *slightly* bigger than the British Empire at its height. BUT only just. AND if you counted all the countries that had *ever* been part of the British Empire, it would cover a larger area than the surface of the moon.

In fact, the British Empire was involved with countries beginning with nearly every letter of the alphabet! The British Empire was massive! Bigger than

INTRODUCTION

a Big Mac. Bigger than Big Ben and Bigfoot. Bigger than the Notorious B.I.G. By 1923, 460 million people were living in the British Empire, or one fifth of the world's population at the time, and, covering some 14 million square miles, it was 150 times the size of Great Britain!

Let's face it, the British Empire is the biggest thing we ever did as a country. Bigger than winning both world wars, bigger than winning any number of World Cups in any number of sports, bigger than inventing James Bond, Harry Potter, Paddington Bear, Peppa Pig and *The Lord of the Rings* combined. Yet we don't talk about it much. It only gets a small mention on the national curriculum, which guides schools on what to teach. And there aren't many films and novels that tell us the story of the British Empire, compared to all the films that have been made about the First and Second World War (and approximately twenty-seven James Bond films, eleven Harry Potter films, six Lord of the Rings films, four Peppa Pig films and three Paddington Bear films).

You might be thinking, *I get it. The empire was big and sounds pretty impressive. But what was it exactly?! And why* should *we be talking about it?* Well, an empire is a collection of nations under the control of another nation or government. Usually the more nations you invade and conquer and 'colonize' (meaning taking over

INTRODUCTION

a place to control it), the more powerful you become. Many leaders throughout history have wanted to create an empire. The Roman Empire, which started in 27 BC and lasted for approximately 500 years, was one of the best known. During this time, the Romans conquered Britain and many other regions in Europe and beyond.

Most people agree that Britain's empire started in about 1600 when Elizabeth I ruled. At the time, Britain ruled over a large portion of Ireland, and lots of seafaring explorers became interested in visiting other countries in search of valuable goods and materials. Britain's empire lasted for some 400 years, and other European nations, including France, Portugal, Spain and the Netherlands (also known as Holland), too had empires around the same time. However, Britain's empire was the largest in history. It was seven times larger than the powerful Roman Empire.

The British ended up colonizing lots of different countries, for lots of different reasons. Sometimes it was to trade in food, spices, cloth and other goods; at other times it was to take British prisoners abroad and leave them in another country. The British also gained control of these nations in lots of different ways. There were times they got control through trade and business, but there were also times they did this through violence. Sometimes they used both methods at the same time.

The British Empire also benefited from the evils of the transatlantic slave trade for a very long time (which I discuss in Chapter 3). If you want to know more about how this all happened, there is further information in my first book on empire for children, *Stolen History*.

So why *don't* we talk about it very much? Well, I've thought about it a lot, and I think one reason is because the British Empire is now largely gone. Apart from fourteen small British-run areas, including Gibraltar in the Mediterranean, the Falkland Islands in the South Atlantic Ocean, and Bermuda in the North Atlantic Ocean, it doesn't really exist. And it's very easy to forget about something that you can no longer see. Like the socks I dropped behind my bed the other day. Or my old collection of Paddington Bear toys.

It might also be because people who are teachers now weren't taught about the British Empire when they were at school, so they don't know how to teach it to children today. I mean, you'd struggle to tell people about how algebra and contour lines worked if you'd not studied them in maths and geography, right?

But I think the main reason we don't talk about the British Empire enough is because it was so complicated.

INTRODUCTION

And as you'll know from facing any difficult work at school, the easiest thing to do in the face of complicated things is to talk about something else instead. Believe me, I've been tempted. I have written several books about the British Empire and sometimes I wish I had chosen to write about Peppa Pig instead.

But we need to understand it and talk about it. Because the British Empire explains a lot of things about the world and Britain. It explains how entire countries like Nigeria and Pakistan came into existence. It explains why many British charities do so much work abroad. It explains some of the racism we see around the world. It explains why Jamaicans eat breadfruit and why Indians drink so much tea. And it partly explains why so many people speak English across the planet.

But how do we even begin to tell this massive story? Almost all the adult books on the topic are incredibly long. Jan Morris, a Welsh historian and author, wrote three books on this subject called Pax Britannica, and they come to well over 1,500 pages in total. My two adult books, *Empireland* and *Empireworld*, run for nearly 800 pages combined.

Luckily for you, this one won't be quite as long. In this book I want to tell you all about what happened through the stories of people travelling through the British

INTRODUCTION

Empire at different times. The journeys I'll talk about are all very different. Sometimes they involved sailing for hundreds or thousands of miles; sometimes they involved walking for hundreds or thousands of miles. Sometimes the people chose to go on their adventures; at others they were forced or tricked into doing so. Sometimes the journeys were taken by people trying to expand the British Empire; sometimes they were trying to stop it in its tracks. Sometimes I'll be describing just one imporant journey that a certain person went on; at other times I'll be describing the many journeys that a particular person went on during their lifetime.

As we go along, I'll also give you examples of things in our modern world that have their roots in the British Empire – foods, places, countries that wouldn't exist at all, or would exist in a different form, if the largest empire in history hadn't happened.

Are you ready to take a trip through the monumental journeys of the British Empire? We'll be travelling both with a king and queen in luxury to India, and a young enslaved man on one of the most brutal journeys in history, on a boat across the Atlantic Ocean. We'll be climbing mountains that had not been climbed before, and visiting lands that people in the West didn't realize even existed. We'll be seeing London through the eyes of an Indigenous

INTRODUCTION

American whose people knew very little about England, and experiencing Tibet through the hostile eyes of some of its first-ever foreign visitors. The one thing all the journeys have in common, though, is that they shaped the British Empire and the future of the world.

CHAPTER 1
The Pirate Queen, c.1530–c.1603

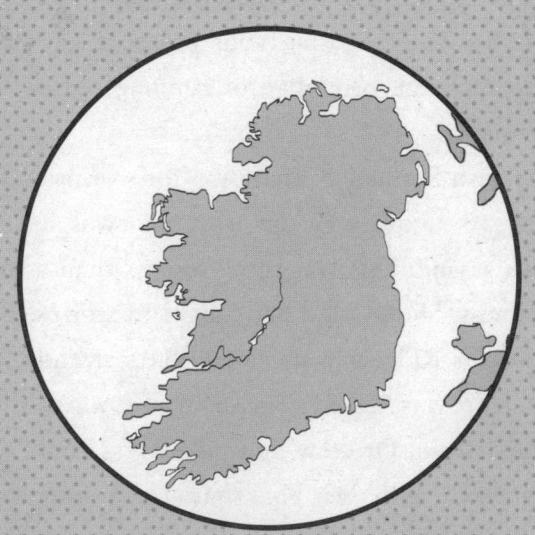

CHAPTER 1

In the twenty-first century it doesn't take long to get from London to Dublin in Ireland: by plane it's a journey of just one hour and twenty minutes. Before the invention of air travel, however, it would take quite a lot longer; a steamship and train in the 1900s would make the journey ten to twelve hours long. Before this, in the 1600s, when people had to travel by sailing ships, and when Ireland was the site of England's first 'colony', it could take an enormous amount of time, between five and fourteen days. And you'd have a lot more to worry about than simply losing your passport, or not being able to recharge your iPad or running out of M&Ms on the plane.

The Irish Sea had a reputation for storms and rough waters. 'As unquiet as the Irish sea' was a common English saying. This was more serious than a touch of seasickness. Ships could get caught in storms; in 1606 Sir Thomas Ridgeway spent two days stranded at sea, as his ship was tossed around by the waves during a perilous storm. Or crew and passengers could even be shipwrecked, with their boat shattering to pieces against rocks, and the people falling overboard.

And then there was the risk of pirates storming the ship, robbing it and perhaps leaving their victims for dead. English, Welsh, Scottish and Irish pirates operated in the Irish Sea, using boats called galleys, which descended from Viking longboats. These boats had both a sail and oars, with two or three men on each oar. Sometimes they captured fishermen and forced them to become pirates themselves.

Now, when I mention pirates, you probably have an image in your mind. After all, they're everywhere, in films like *Pirates of the Caribbean*, in books like *Treasure Island*, in video games like *Assassin's Creed IV*. There's Captain Jack Sparrow. Captain Hook. Long John Silver. Blackbeard. And then there's the infamous pirate who reportedly buried a lot of fabulous treasure that has never been found, and who was hanged and his body left rotting over the River Thames as a warning to others not to follow his path. His name was Captain Kidd.

What these pirates have in common – whether they are real or from books and films – is that they are typically seen as rebels and crooks. And, of course, they are all men. The fact is, though, that not all pirates who attacked and robbed ships at sea were rebels. So-called 'privateers' did the same kind of thieving but with the permission of the authorities. Often the only difference between a privateer and a pirate was a piece of paper, a letter from a king, for example, giving them permission

CHAPTER 1

to rob the ships of enemy nations, as long as they gave some of their profits to the authorities.

Also, not all pirates were men. A surprising number of women roamed the seas, and I want to tell you about one in particular, who is perhaps the bravest and most impressive of the lot, and who was active at an early stage of the British Empire. Gráinne O'Malley, also known as Grace O'Malley, was born around 1530 and, as you might guess from her name, was Irish. Gráinne was born into a wealthy family in the part of the country known as County Mayo (in case you were wondering, no, there is no County Ketchup). Her family, or 'clan', owned several castles, and were also big into seafaring. Their motto was 'Powerful by land and by sea'. What would your family motto be? I think ours would be 'No, YOU'RE sitting on the remote control!'

Gráinne learned about life on the high seas from a young age. And by that I mean around your age. Imagine! Rather than going to school, she was learning about tying knots and swashbuckling. I don't know what swashbuckling involves, but it sounds more interesting than PSHE. However, even then there were some journeys that were seen as unsuitable for girls. Legend has it that when her father refused to take her on one such trip, saying he could only take her brother, Gráinne dressed as a boy and cut off all her hair. Because of this, her brother gave her the nickname 'Gráinne Mhaoul', which means 'Bald Grace' in Irish, and over time this led to her becoming known as 'Granuaile'.

There are lots of stories about Gráinne like this, which may or may not be true. She was the kind of extraordinary person who inspired legends and myths. I'm sure you know someone (indeed, it might be you!) who is always getting up to exciting things. Their friends are always saying, 'Have you heard what so-and-so has done now?' Well, that was Gráinne.

I just want to take you back for a moment at this point, to fill you in on the background to Gráinne's story. Some *historical context* if you will. That sounds dull, I know, but it's important, and I'll make it as interesting as I can. When Gráinne was born, Ireland had been ruled by the English for about 360 years, after it was invaded by the Anglo-Normans who made up the ruling class of England. (The Normans were a group of people who descended from Vikings and settled in Normandy, France, in the 900s. The Normans invaded England in the year 1066.)

Ireland has been called 'the first colony' of England. But the English were only really interested in the city of Dublin and a few other towns. For most people in the

CHAPTER 1

rest of the country life went on as it always had done, following old Irish traditions.

Then Henry VIII became the king of England. When he wasn't busy getting married, getting divorced or chopping people's heads off (including those of his wives), he worried about the threats that England faced. Because there had recently been a rebellion in Ireland against English rule, he decided Ireland was one of those threats. So in 1542 he made himself king of Ireland too, and demanded that the clans there pledged themselves to him. When Henry died, his son, Edward VI, and then his daughter, Elizabeth I, continued with this mission. If clans resisted, they risked their property being attacked or stolen by the English.

You may know that during Henry VIII's reign the official religion of England became a huge hot topic. *Very* simply put, England went from being mostly Catholic to being mostly Protestant. And both sides got extremely upset about it. It was *possibly* a bit like how angry both sides get when Wolverhampton Wanderers (the best team in the world) play West Bromwich (the worst team in the world). But with bells on, because those who were on the 'wrong' side of the argument had a fairly high risk of being beheaded or burned at the stake.

Ireland was very firmly Catholic, which made the

Irish even more reluctant to show loyalty to the English. And adding to the tension was the fact that Spain and France (who were also firmly Catholic) wanted to use Ireland as a base to invade England.

Now let's go back to where we left Gráinne. At the age of sixteen she married the son of another powerful clan leader and the pair had children together. (They married young in those days.) But her life was about to take a turn for the unusual. First, her husband was killed by a rival clan. The Irish tradition was that a dead man's family should give his widow a portion of his wealth, but her husband's family refused. So, in order to support herself and her family, Gráinne decided to turn to piracy.

As I mentioned above, in Gráinne's time, people didn't view pirates in the same way we do today. Modern-day pirates can now face a life in prison in places like the USA, and even the death penalty in other countries. To say that piracy was a respectable job in Gráinne's day is perhaps going a bit far, but it was quite common and the authorities would sometimes tolerate it – especially if they were getting a cut of the loot!

Gráinne lived in a castle and ran a kind of pirate business empire. Over her long career, she commanded many ships, and an army of 200 fighting men. She traded things like barrels of salted fish and cattle hides

CHAPTER 1

with Spain in return for things such as iron, weapons and wine. She took hired soldiers (called mercenaries) from Scotland to Ireland, and carried out cattle raids (stealing animals in large numbers) on nearby areas. She and her team also patrolled the sea and attacked passing ships, taking money or other valuables from them, as well as defending the coast against enemy ships.

Gráinne's toughness and cleverness can be illustrated by another of the 'did you hear what Gráinne did?' stories. One of her castles, which was on a small island, was attacked by English soldiers. In response, Gráinne ordered her men to remove the lead from the castle roof, melt it down and pour the molten metal on to the soldiers below. She then sent a messenger through a secret passage from the island to the mainland to summon her fleet to come and save her.

She married again in 1566, and had a son called Tibbot in 1567. Another legend says that she gave birth to little baby Tibbot while she was at sea, and when he was less than an hour old, Algerian pirates boarded the ship. Gráinne calmly wrapped her newborn son in a blanket, went up on deck and rallied her crew to capture the attacking vessel. In short, she was a total badass, and, as an English lord wrote at the time, 'a notorious woman in all the coasts of Ireland'.

CHAPTER 1

But it wasn't an easy life. In 1577, she was arrested and sent to prison in Dublin Castle. She was only allowed out once she had promised to give up being a pirate. But she couldn't stop!

Then, when a stern new English governor was appointed and he and Gráinne did not see eye to eye, she was, at the age of fifty-six, imprisoned again and was *almost* executed. Of course there's another one of those 'did you hear ...?' stories about her near-death experience. Apparently, *just* before she was sent to her death, she was freed. We don't know for sure what happened. One biographer, Anne Chambers, suggests that her husband rebelled and that Gráinne was released to keep the peace. Another rumour suggests that Queen Elizabeth ordered her release, and that she was saved by the sound of galloping hooves and a messenger. Very dramatic!

Tragically, though she had been spared death, things then went downhill for Gráinne. The English governor of Connacht, Sir Richard Bingham, was determined to crush her. In 1586, Bingham's brother, Captain John Bingham, seized the lands of Gráinne's son Owen, captured him and eighteen of his followers, and killed them all. Then he arrested her brother and Tibbot. Next he took Gráinne's cattle and seized her ships.

These terrible events left her very short of money. In the end, she had to write to Elizabeth I, begging for help in getting her property back. The two women, queen and pirate, met at Greenwich Palace in 1593. Gráinne promised to give up her piracy and pledged allegiance to Queen Elizabeth if she helped her get her property back and secure the release of Tibbot and her brother. Queen Elizabeth agreed to her terms, and Gráinne promised to 'invade with sword and fire all Your Highness's enemies'. For some years she worked with the colonizers with whom she had fought in the past, and continued to defend Ireland at the same time. Gráinne died a decade later, in about 1603.

There's a social media website and app called Facebook, which you might not have heard of as it's now pretty much only used by old people. The reason I'm telling you about this is because on Facebook there's a feature that lets you tell your friends what your relationship status is. You can say if you're single, married, divorced, or if it's complicated. If Facebook had been around in the sixteenth century, I think Gráinne would definitely have chosen this last option for her relationship with the English.

The fact that she fought the English colonizers of Ireland but also worked with them has made her a tricky

CHAPTER 1

subject for some in the years since. Some people would prefer to see her purely as a hero who fought for Irish independence against the English. But there's more to her story than this. I think Gráinne's story is a reminder that we should not be too quick to judge people from history from where we sit today. Rather, we should view her actions in *context* (that word again!). The English were a larger, stronger force than the Irish, and so she may have come to believe that fighting them was a battle she could never win. Or maybe, by working with both, she was trying to help the two sides find common ground.

Gráinne also had her children and the rest of her clan to think about. She needed to look after them. And, at a time when women weren't given many options in life, Gráinne was extremely brave, independent, fierce and resourceful. And, most important of all, she was a PIRATE! She wouldn't let ANYBODY tell her what to do!

From sailing the seas, defending the coast and fighting the queen's enemies, I think what we *can* all agree on is that her life was packed with dangerous journeys and exciting adventures. I mean, did you *hear* what Gráinne did . . .?

THE USA

America and Britain can seem like very different places. America's national foods are things like hamburgers and hot dogs, and Britain's are fish and chips, and curry. Americans are usually quite direct in the way they speak, whereas British people are so polite that they will say 'sorry' to someone who has stood on *their* foot on the bus. The USA is the largest economy in the world, and Britain is not.

Indeed, I think most proud Americans do not like to think of their homeland as a legacy of the British Empire. After all, they famously kicked out the British colonizers in the late eighteenth century, during the War of Independence. You might notice that in a fair number of Hollywood films, the baddie is often played by a British actor. How about Saruman in *The Lord of the Rings*, the sheriff of Nottingham in *Robin Hood: Prince of Thieves*, Scar in the 1994 film of *The Lion King*, or Shere Khan in *The Jungle Book*? I'm convinced

CHAPTER 1

this is because Americans associate the British accent with bad things they want to get rid of.

But the truth is, there's a lot that can be explained about the USA by the fact it was once under British control. Firstly, and most obviously, the national language is English. There are also certain legal, political and economic systems that were taken from the British - I don't think you'd thank me for going into lots of detail on these, so just trust me that they're kind of important, and they came with the Puritans.

You may have heard of Puritans before but not know exactly who or what they were. They were English and strict Protestants who were disappointed with the Church of England, which they saw as weak and corrupt. So, when the opportunity arose to start again in the New World (the area we now call South, Central and North America), they grabbed it. In 1630, a shipload of Puritans reached Massachusetts, and established the town of Boston.

Over the following years, 21,000 Puritans settled in the place they named New England. But before this there were many Indigenous Americans who had been living on this land for ages. ('Indigenous' is the name given to the people who were originally living there before colonists arrived.) So you may be thinking, how was there room for everyone?

Well, not long after the first settlers arrived, the area around Massachusetts was destroyed by a series of devastating diseases, which were almost certainly brought in by the settlers who were arriving from foreign lands. These diseases killed many people in the Indigenous American

CHAPTER 1

community. As much as ninety per cent of the population died. It was this tragic event that made it possible for the Puritans to settle so successfully in New England.

The Puritans saw North America as a promised land where they could flourish. The destruction of the Indigenous American population was taken as a sign from God that they were on the right path. And, indeed, they got to work repopulating the land with their own people. By the end of the twentieth century, there were 16 million descendants of these 'chosen people'. And, at the same time, millions of Irish people relocated to the USA as well, because famine, which had been made worse by the British, made life at home impossible.

So if the British Empire hadn't happened, both the population and the culture of the USA would be very different. The idea that the USA is completely free of British influence is simply not

THE PIRATE QUEEN, c.1530–c.1603

true! There, I said it. Now maybe I should watch out for a new Hollywood film featuring an English baddie called Satan Sanghera!

CHAPTER 2
The True Story of Pocahontas, 1616–17

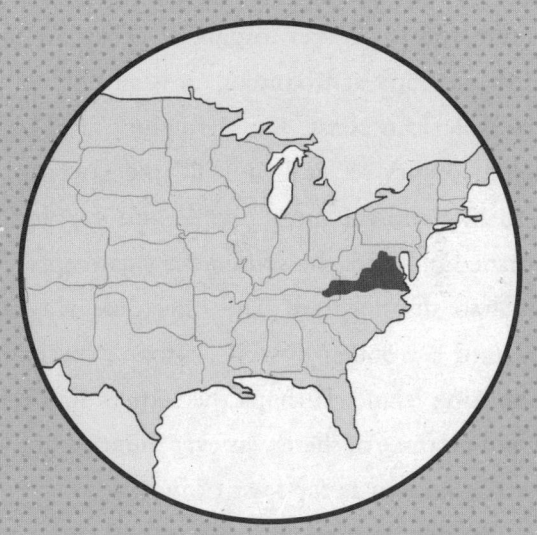

CHAPTER 2

By the late 1500s and early 1600s, England was in the grip of a fever. Colonization fever. They had watched the Spanish conquer much of the New World and find vast amounts of gold in the process. As we just saw on page 22, England, in addition to the territories they already had in places like Ireland, wanted a piece of the action. But English efforts to colonize North America actually began several decades before the Puritans arrived. It was Elizabeth I who got the ball rolling, sending her favourite explorer Sir Walter Raleigh to lay claim to the region.

In the 1580s, Walter organized two attempts to establish a colony at Roanoke, an island off the north-eastern American coast. But the colony of 115 people struggled to survive, and in 1587 the governor sailed back to England for more people and supplies. When he returned in 1590, the settlement was empty. All 115 people had disappeared! The only clue was a word carved into a wooden post: 'Croatoan', the name of a neighbouring island. Perhaps the settlers had relocated there, but no trace of them was ever found, and Roanoke came to be known as the Lost Colony.

This was not a very promising start, and, unsurprisingly, the English didn't rush to try again. I might not have been tempted either. Besides, over the next decade England was busy fighting Spain. It was only after peace was finally declared in 1604 that Elizabeth I's successor, King James I, turned his attention to colonization in North America. In 1606, James issued a royal charter to set up the Virginia Company. Their job was to establish an English colony in North America and to profit from its precious metals and resources.

On 20 December 1606, three ships set sail from England: the *Discovery*, *Godspeed* and *Susan Constant* with 144 men and boys on board in total. We know the names of four boys – Samuel Collier, Nathaniel Peacock, James Brumfield and Richard Mutton. They might have been orphans or from poor families, who were old enough to work, perhaps around the age of twelve. Other passengers included six carpenters, two surgeons, two bricklayers, a tailor, a barber and a drummer!

The voyage lasted over four months. About halfway through, one of the men on the ships, John Smith, was arrested for plotting a rebellion. He was to be executed on arrival in America. But, luckily for John, when they reached Virginia, the captain opened some sealed orders from the company, which named John as one of the colony's leaders. So he narrowly escaped death! Not unlike Gráinne's rumoured escape in the last chapter!

The settlers chose a site on land belonging to the Pamunkey tribe. They named the settlement Jamestown

CHAPTER 2

after the king (for more on the origins of place names, see page 41). I guess the modern equivalent would be coming across a new planet and naming it Starmercury, after the current British prime minister. They were excited to find nearby forests for timber and a shiny metal that looked like gold. But when two of the ships headed back to England with a load of the shiny metal, it turned out to be a worthless material called iron pyrite! Awkward.

The settlers found life difficult in Jamestown. They had chosen a marshy, unproductive site for their settlement and started to fall ill. They depended on the local Indigenous Americans for food, but this was a time of terrible drought and food supplies ran short. At first the settlers and the local Pamunkey chief, Powhatan, had a friendly relationship. But things quickly turned violent. John Smith led expeditions to trade for food, and on one trip he was captured by Powhatan's brother and taken to the chief's headquarters in the village of Werowocomoco. Years later John claimed that his life was saved by Powhatan's favourite daughter Pocahontas.

And if this particular name and story sound familiar, it's because what happened is a famous story, made even more famous through a cartoon movie made by Disney called *Pocahontas*, about an Indigenous American princess who falls in love with an Englishman in the

CHAPTER 2

seventeenth century. If you've seen it, I'd forgive you for thinking you had watched a true story. After all, the story revolves around John Smith and Pocahontas, who really did exist. Admittedly 'John Smith' sounds made up – 'Quick, film writer, think of a name that sounds really English!' – but that actually was his real name. It's also true, as the film shows, that John was taken captive.

But – and I hope this won't come as too much of a shock to you – cartoons aren't real. If you've picked up a book about history, I trust you're ready to deal with the fact that there isn't a real person called Homer Simpson living in a real town called Springfield, with a real son called Bart who enjoys nothing more than telling people to 'Eat my shorts!' And (spoiler alert!) there's not much history in Disney's *Pocahontas* that is true. Not least that while the cartoon movie calls her 'Pocahontas', this was just a nickname, meaning 'playful one' or, when she was being more annoying, 'ill-behaved child'. She had two real names: Amonute and Matoaka. Imagine having two real names and then still having a nickname! (And she took a fourth name later on!) I don't know about you, but I'm feeling lacking in the name department.

Also, while there is one portrait of her towards the end of her life, we don't know what Pocahontas looked like as a young person, and she probably didn't look *anything* like how Disney portrayed her. Disney have made her look really quite grown up when the real Pocahontas was, at the time of the story, a child – somewhere between ten and twelve years old!

The biggest problem of all (yet another spoiler alert!) is the love story between John Smith and Pocahontas at the heart of the cartoon. Lots of historians don't believe that Pocahontas saved John Smith's life, as he claimed, let alone that there was a romance between them. You can see why John Smith would spread a story about being saved, whether it was true or not. It made him look special!

And other English people liked the story too. North America was a large and important part of the British Empire until the Americans got rid of the British and left the empire in the late 1700s. This story supported two ideas – one, that the colonizers were welcomed and admired by some Indigenous Americans, and two, that some Indigenous Americans could be violent if you weren't careful.

It helped create the sense that the British Empire was a happy place, when in reality it often involved the British being brutally violent to indigenous people and facing lots of resistance. And so people kept on telling

CHAPTER 2

the story of John Smith being saved. At some point someone added the idea that Pocahontas was in love with John Smith to give it an even better ending, and over time it seemed to become a fact. It's a good example of how in history if something is repeated often enough, it can become widely believed, even though there is no real proof for it. We sometimes call this a *myth*.

The ending of the film is another problem. It concludes with John sailing away, leaving a broken-hearted Pocahontas behind in her magical homeland with her pet raccoon and a talking tree. In reality, not only do trees not talk, but lots of the English stayed there and claimed Virginia as an English colony. Just as its capital was named after King James I, Virginia was named after the Virgin Queen, as Elizabeth I had been known. Meanwhile, Pocahontas actually ended up buried in ... England.

You see, she had quite a life, much more interesting and complicated than the one described in the cartoon. It's rare that the true story is more dramatic than the film! Apparently Pocahontas had a lot of tattoos, which were common in her nation, and was very good at doing cartwheels! She was married very young, between thirteen and fifteen years old, but some historians believe this first husband was killed. Soon afterwards, Pocahontas was taken hostage by an Englishman called Captain Samuel Argall, when she was tricked into boarding his boat. The people who tricked her were rewarded by Argall with the present of a 'small copper kettle'. Not a gift that features high on your birthday lists, I imagine. Argall's plan was to capture Pocahontas in order to force her father, Powhatan, to release some Englishmen he had taken prisoner.

Now this is where things get really dark. Because following the kidnapping, rather than returning to Werowocomoco, Pocahontas was taken to Jamestown to live among the English colonists. She changed her religion to Christianity (the term for this is *converted*), changed her name to Rebecca, and married an Englishman called John Rolfe (almost every other Englishman was also called John back then but Rolfe was a particularly well-known John who helped to create the tobacco trade in North America). Are you thinking, wait, what? Why would Pocahontas choose to leave her tribe and join the people who had stolen their land and kidnapped her?

In the centuries since, people have debated why Pocahontas might have done this. Those who are fans of European colonization argue it was because she loved and admired English people so much that she decided to leave her old way of life and become one of them.

CHAPTER 2

And so, they say, it's a good thing they colonized the Indigenous American lands. This explanation feeds into the myth that she was in love with John Smith.

Other accounts, from Indigenous American sources, say that Pocahontas did not decide to live among the white colonizers because she admired them so much. Instead, she had been kidnapped and had no choice in the matter. She had been treated brutally and violently, and had to have an Englishman's baby. Also, we need to remember that there would have been a cruel trend for English explorers to take 'human pets' back to England from 'exotic' parts of North and South America, the Caribbean, Africa and Asia to demonstrate how they would cope with English life.

We might never know all the things that happened to Pocahontas. But we do know how her story ended. Pocahontas spent nine months in England in 1616–17. She travelled there on a trip organized by the Virginia Company to show the British public how successful their venture was. Because her father was such an important leader, the English wanted to show her off as a princess and as the first Indigenous American who had converted to Christianity. The party was made up of eleven other members of the Pamunkey tribe including Uttamatomakkin, who was Pocahontas's brother-in-law, and four women. Two members of the party stayed in England for at least five years.

As an Indigenous American princess, Pocahontas attended several court events (though her husband, John, a mere farmer, was not invited). Wearing the clothes of a fancy English lady, Pocahontas even met King James I and Queen Anne, but apparently she was very unimpressed by the king's appearance and didn't realize who he was! During her time in London, Pocahontas had her portrait painted by a Dutch artist who later made an engraving

of her in English dress. This helped to promote the image of Pocahontas as a grand and powerful princess.

Tragically Pocahontas never saw her home again. At the start of her voyage back to Virginia, when the boat was still on the River Thames near London, she fell ill and died. Some people think that she might have been poisoned, as she died just after having dinner with Captain Argall, the same man who is said to have tricked her on to the boat and kidnapped her years before. Others think she probably died of natural causes.

She was only about twenty-one years old. She must have known that her short life had been quite extraordinary, but imagine if she had been told that, 400 years later, she would be world famous and the star of a Disney cartoon.

While the cartoon is inaccurate, it does explain some useful things about this phase of the British Empire in this part of the world, particularly through its catchiest and darkest song – 'Savages'. Forget the inspirational message of, say, *Frozen*'s 'Let It Go' – the 'Savages' song is from the bit in the story when the two sides want to kill and destroy each other, and talk about one another in horrible ways. I can tell you that walking around the supermarket chanting 'Savages! Savages! Barely even human!' gets you funny looks. But the lyrics tell us something about the brutal racism of colonization in North America.

It tells us that the English settlers often had very racist attitudes towards Indigenous Americans, describing them as 'filthy little heathens', a 'disgusting race' and 'only good when dead'. This awful way of seeing and talking about other human beings made it easier for the colonizers to kill Indigenous Americans to get them out of their way. They died in enormous numbers after the English arrived. In the territory that would become British North America, the Indigenous American population had stood at about 560,000 in the year 1500. By 1700, there were fewer than half that number.

Meanwhile, the way that Pocahontas might have died in real life tells us something else about this history. We don't know for sure what killed her, but a disease such as smallpox or tuberculosis is possible. Indigenous people usually didn't have natural protection from the infectious diseases that existed in other countries, just as you wouldn't have natural protection from diseases from parts of the world you've not visited. Their bodies hadn't had time to build up 'immunity'. And it was disease, rather than violence, that had the biggest impact on indigenous populations when the European colonizers arrived.

CHAPTER 2

Some scientists even argue that British efforts to colonize that part of the world would have been unsuccessful had it not been for the diseases the Europeans took with them. Between 1616 and 1619 the Massachusetts Bay area in North America was ravaged by a deadly disease – probably smallpox or viral hepatitis – which killed as many as ninety per cent of the people who lived there. And horribly, as we learned on page 24, the religious English colonizers saw deaths such as these as a sign from God that they were doing the right thing. In 1634, John Winthrop, the first governor of the Massachusetts Bay colony, claimed: 'For the natives, they are neere all dead of small Poxe, so as the Lord hathe cleared our title to what we possess.'

PLACE NAMES

Let's have a quiz. How many places called *Plymouth* do you think there are in the world? Yes, there's that one in south-west England, with all the ships. But there must be more than that, otherwise I wouldn't ask. How many more? Fifty-three! Who guessed that? You? Well done! There are at least fifty-three. (To be honest, I stopped counting after this.)

And how many places called *York*? Thirty-five? Yes, at least that many!

And how about *Birmingham*? At least eighteen? Quite right!

And *Victoria*? Simply loads of those. More than eighty, you say? Gosh, you're amazing at this.

We could continue, but I think you get the idea. British place names can be found all over the world and are a direct legacy of its empire. Many of them are in America. In fact, someone

CHAPTER 2

once told me that on his drive from the state of Pennsylvania to the state of Maryland, he passed through Reading, Lancaster, York, Shrewsbury and Hereford – all of which are named after British towns and cities!

Plymouth was a popular one, because the Pilgrim Fathers famously set sail from Plymouth to make their homes in the New World. These people were a group of religious rebels who left England to escape persecution for their Protestant beliefs – they were extreme Puritans who wanted to worship in a way that was not approved of by the Church of England. Plymouth Colony in Massachusetts was the second English settlement in America. (The first was Jamestown in Virginia (see page 29) – there are at least forty-one more Jamestowns around the world too!)

It's curious that after long, tough journeys colonists named the places they 'discovered' after the places or monarchs they had left behind.

Were they just unimaginative? Or too excited and distracted by their adventure to think up an original name? Perhaps that came into it a bit. But I think they also wanted to claim ownership of these conquered lands, and the names were like a stamp saying 'property of Britain'.

This desire even extended beyond Earth and into space! When the British astronomer William Herschel discovered a new planet while stargazing in his garden, he named it Georgium Sidus, or 'George's Star', after King George III. The rest of the world wasn't so keen on it, so the name was eventually changed to Uranus and instead became the butt of many a classroom joke.

Other places have been renamed in recent years, to try to move on from their colonial pasts. Many of these places are in India and were named by the British. For instance, the British named the Indian city of Bombay; now it is called Mumbai. Calcutta is now Kolkata.

CHAPTER 2

> One thing that really stands out to me in all this naming is that, to my knowledge, no one has ever named another place after my hometown of Wolverhampton. Can you believe it? Maybe I'll have to take up stargazing and find a distant new star to name Wulfrunian Sidus.

CHAPTER 3
The Travels of Olaudah Equiano, c.1745–97

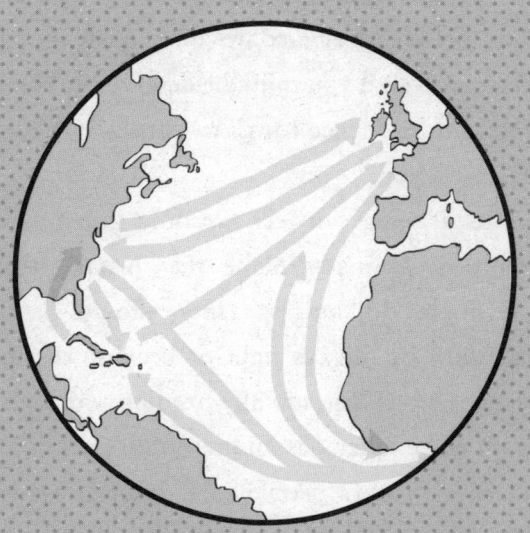

CHAPTER 3

There is nothing historians like more than a good old argument. Almost every time I, or any other historian, says something about some point of history, you can bet someone will reply, 'I think you'll find that . . .' and then claim the opposite. Actually their reply is often less polite than that!

Though arguments over history aren't quite the same as the arguments you have with your brother about how Coco Pops are better than Crunchy Nut cornflakes. To win the argument, it's not enough to say 'because I like them' or 'because they just are' or to push your brother off his chair, even if you think he deserves it. You need to give facts and evidence to try to persuade other people to agree with you.

All this arguing can feel tiresome sometimes. Some historians occasionally make the mistake that your parents might do, and say they should be believed because they are always right or because they're older and know better! But actually arguing – or *debating* if you want to be fancy – is an important part of studying history. When lots of people have different views on an important subject and have to explain and defend their ideas, the subject ends up being talked about and studied in detail.

Eventually one point of view usually 'wins' and

becomes widely accepted. But then sometimes new evidence comes out and the debates start all over again. That's how writing history is supposed to work. And so historians will probably always be arguing about who was the most important American president, or what was the real cause of the First World War, or what people ate in the Stone Age, or if Pocahontas saved John Smith from death or whatever. It keeps them busy. There are, though, some things in history that almost everyone agrees upon without (much) squabbling. This is what is called a *consensus*. And one of those things is that the Middle Passage – the next journey we are going to learn about – was utterly horrible.

The Middle Passage was a sea voyage that took place many thousands of times in the period between 1514 and the mid-nineteenth century. On these journeys enslaved people were taken from countries across Africa to European colonies in America and the West Indies. This involved taking Black men, women and children, who had been kidnapped from their homes, and shipping them across the Atlantic Ocean to force them to complete gruelling work on farms, for free. More than 3 million people from the continent of Africa suffered this fate on British ships. To be on those ships meant that, whether you were a child or an adult, you

CHAPTER 3

had most likely been separated from your family forever, and were being taken to a strange country where, unless you were extremely lucky, you would be forced to do back-breaking work in terrible heat for no pay until the day you died.

It was called the Middle Passage because it was the central section of a three-part slave-trading route called the Triangular Trade. British enslavers sailed to West Africa from ports such as London, Liverpool and Bristol. Enslaved people were bought there for supplies like textiles, alcohol, iron and guns. After that, the enslaved people were shipped across the Atlantic to be sold in British territories in North America and the West Indies. The boats then returned to England with a cargo of rice, tobacco and other items to sell.

The conditions on the ship were worse than you can possibly imagine. The Middle Passage journey took

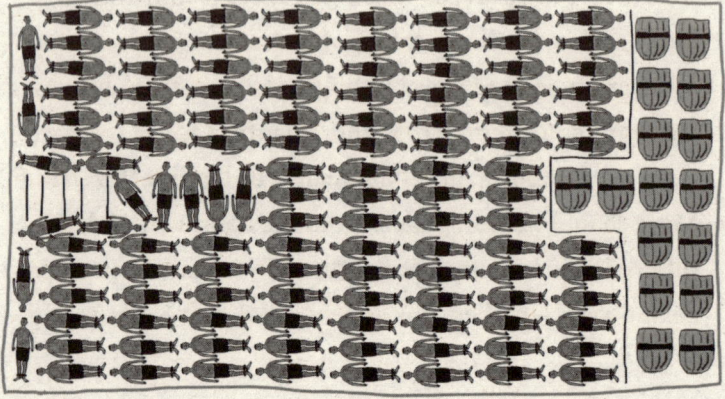

between twenty-one and ninety days, depending on the weather. Each ship was hugely overcrowded and the enslaved were kept lying down, crammed in tight rows below the deck, often chained up so they couldn't stand up or even turn over. Remember, however, that the fate of these enslaved people was to be sold as workers, and their captors wanted them to arrive alive and fit, so they could fetch a good price. So sometimes they would be taken out on deck and forced to 'dance' – jump up and down – so their muscles did not waste away.

Disease spread quickly, and a significant number of people on the Middle Passage – historians estimate between ten and fifteen per cent – died before arriving in the New World. Tragically their bodies were thrown overboard into the shark-infested waters. When up on deck, many people suffered extreme violence at the hands of their captors. It is probable they did not know that, at the other end of their voyage, an even worse fate awaited them – they would be enslaved for the rest of their lives. I know this is all truly horrible, but it's important that everyone knows the grim truth about the slave trade.

We know some facts about the Middle Passage from records and accounts left by the enslavers who ran the ships. However, the key evidence that tells us what it was actually like to be transported below deck comes from the *first-hand* accounts of enslaved people who survived the crossing. One of the most famous of these survivors is an extraordinary man called Olaudah Equiano. He wrote a book, *The Interesting Narrative of the Life of Olaudah Equiano; or, Gustavus Vassa, the African, Written by Himself* (book titles were often not very snappy in those days), which helped to wake the world up to the evils of the slave trade.

In the book, Olaudah tells us how he was born in 1745 in Essaka, in the Kingdom of Benin, located in present-day Nigeria (see page 109). When he was eleven, slave traders attacked his village, and he and his little sister were kidnapped. They were eventually separated, never to see each other again, and Olaudah was transported to the West Indies on the Middle Passage. He had never seen the sea before – nor a white person. He describes the 'brutal cruelty' on the ship, his fear of his vicious captors, the open tubs used as toilets below deck that children sometimes fell into, and the terrible smell they were forced to live with.

From the West Indies, Olaudah was transported to Virginia, where he was sold three times to different slave owners. Unlike most enslaved people, who spent their lives working on large farms called plantations, he mostly worked aboard ships – unpaid, of course – including with the Royal Navy. His job was as a powder monkey, which sounds like it could possibly be quite fun but was actually very dangerous. He had to supply the ship's cannons with gunpowder during battles. And there was always a risk that everything could blow up, including him!

Olaudah became the property of a naval captain, who gave him a new name, Gustavus Vassa, and Olaudah fought alongside him in the Seven Years War against France. This was the first global war; on one side were Great Britain, Hanover and Prussia (old countries that now cover modern Germany, Poland, and part of Russia); on the other was an alliance of France, Austria, Sweden, Saxony (now part of modern Germany), Russia and Spain. He saw lots of terrible violence.

In 1766, Olaudah did something very few enslaved people were ever in a position to do – he bought his freedom. Having made money through trading in things like fruit and glass on his travels, he offered his owner £40 (approximately £7,000 in today's money) to release him. He described the moment of freedom: 'my feet scarcely touched the ground, for they were winged with joy'.

As a free man, Olaudah continued to work on ships, and led a life filled with journeys and adventures. This included travelling to the Arctic, and he was possibly the first Black man ever to do so. During the journey the men were attacked by walruses and were forced to hunt polar

CHAPTER 3

bears to survive! Also on the trip was someone called Horatio Nelson. He was a British navy commander, who became a hero during the Napoleonic Wars in which Britain fought France. Nelson was killed at the Battle of Trafalgar in 1805, and there is a famous statue of him on a very tall column in the centre of London.

Olaudah also sailed to Naples in Italy, where he witnessed the volcano Mount Vesuvius erupting. His ship was covered in a thick layer of ash. Eventually he left his life on the seas and settled in England, was baptised at the age of around twelve, and devoted himself to the campaign to end slavery (this is called the *abolitionist movement*). He was involved in the effort to set up a colony for freed slaves in Sierra Leone, and was one of the founders of Sons of Africa, the first Black political organization in Britain, made up of formerly enslaved people.

In 1789, he published his book. He promoted and sold it himself, which meant he kept all the profits. And it became a sensation! It was translated into many languages and made him good money. As well as detailing the horrors of the Middle Passage and his time in slavery, the book was praised for Olaudah's lively, warm portrayal of the customs and rituals of his village life in Benin. This was important because those involved in the

THE TRAVELS OF OLAUDAH EQUIANO, c.1745–97

slave trade often justified their business by *dehumanizing* the African people. They made out that African lives had little meaning and that they lived more like animals than humans. Olaudah's portrayal of village life made it clear that life in Africa was rich and meaningful, despite what colonists had led people to believe.

Olaudah married an English woman and they had two daughters. He died in 1797 at the age of fifty-two. Ten years later, trading enslaved people in the British Empire was finally abolished. Although he did not live to see that momentous day, he must have known that he

CHAPTER 3

had massively helped the cause. So often powerful white people are given all the credit for abolishing slavery, and it's important to remember that formerly enslaved people like Olaudah played a role in this too.

Now, over two centuries later, all right-minded people agree that the slave trade was a terrible evil. The misery suffered by those on the Middle Passage is not in question. However, there *is* an argument attached to the story of Olaudah Equiano. Some historians question where he was really born and if his book was entirely a first-hand account, or perhaps a story that mixed together various people's experiences. I don't know the truth. This is one argument that I have not been involved in! But I think the really interesting question is – does it matter?

Does it matter if Olaudah's eye-opening story is not entirely his first-hand experience? If he himself had not been crammed, terrified, in the stinking darkness below deck on the Middle Passage? Maybe he had heard what it was like from other enslaved people who *had* been kidnapped from Africa and taken to America, and decided to tell their story as if it was his own. He might have decided that this would be a better way of helping to bring about the end of slavery in the British Empire.

After all, most enslaved people were not able to buy their freedom or have the time to write a book, as he did. Few of them wrote brilliantly in English, as he did, because they were rarely allowed an education. Olaudah had a voice that most other enslaved people did not have, and perhaps he realized the world might listen to him. It *might* not have been *his* truth, but it was certainly the truth of many others; we have plenty of evidence for that. It's possible he thought the end justified the means, which means that if a goal is important enough, then it's OK to use any method you can to achieve it. And it would be fair to argue that there is no more important goal than ending the slave trade.

Perhaps this could be a subject for your next school debate. A lot of historians do think Olaudah's story is what really happened to him, but how much do *you* think it matters?

In the meantime, I'd like to make a suggestion for something to do if you are ever in London. Go to the British Museum and find the Africa Galleries. There you can see a selection of precious objects from the historical kingdom of Benin. This includes the Benin Bronzes, a group of metal sculptures made around the 1500s. They are very beautiful and intricate, and would've taken much skill and creativity to make. They provide clear

CHAPTER 3

evidence that Benin was a highly developed, cultured society. Just as Olaudah said it was in his book, two centuries later.

The Benin Bronzes are also controversial, because they were looted, meaning stolen by force, from Benin by British troops in 1897, and some people think they should be given back, or *repatriated*. Indeed, lots of smaller museums and private collectors who have similar items have already sent them back. Should the British Museum do the same? Now this *is* an argument that I have been involved in. But I'll spare you – for now!

SPORT

Anyone for a game of croquet?

Yes, you at the back, you have a question?

What *is* croquet? Fair enough. Croquet is hardly popular in the playground these days. So, for those who don't know, croquet is a game played on lawns, and it involves carefully hitting heavy balls through hoops with a mallet (a long-handled wooden stick with a head like a hammer).

Still no takers? OK then. How about a spot of footie?

Now we're talking. Look at all those hands in the air!

If you love football, you're not alone. But did you know that the reason this sport is so popular across the world is largely due to the British Empire? Yes, Britain was the pioneer of the planet's favourite

CHAPTER 3

ball game. The authors of the book *How Britain Brought Football to the World* claim that the British were directly involved in the beginnings of football in well over 100 countries around the globe.

You might say that football is the British Empire's greatest legacy. Except if you're into cricket. Or tennis. Or horse racing. Or rugby (which evolved into American football in the United States). Or, indeed, croquet! Because the worldwide popularity of all those sports is also largely down to the British Empire.

Although football is now by far more popular worldwide, cricket is the game that is most strongly associated with Britain's imperial past. Nowadays if a country is really good at cricket, it's almost always because it was once part of the British Empire. Think of India, Sri Lanka, Pakistan and Australia.

The reason the British spread these games wherever they went around the globe was not just to keep themselves amused – although that was definitely part of it. There was also a belief that these games were a good way of encouraging 'imperial values'. By this I mean that the British thought that the character traits needed to be good at sport – such as a sense of fair play, staying calm and performing well under pressure, and being a team player – were typically British traits. And they believed they were encouraging these values in the populations of the places they colonized by introducing these sports.

Interestingly, the phrase 'to be a good sport', which you may be familiar with, means something slightly different. It means to be polite and respectful even when you lose. This is definitely something the British have had to learn – almost all the countries they introduced these sports to now beat them in tournaments! The only exception to this is the most prestigious croquet title in the world, the MacRobertson International Croquet Shield, which is held by England.

CHAPTER 4

Banks and Cook's Voyage to the South Pacific, 1768–71

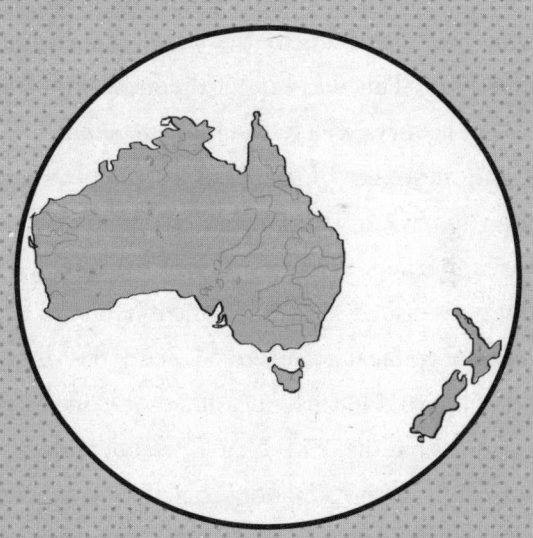

CHAPTER 4

Note to self: do not go on about breadfruit!

Oh, am I speaking out loud? I should explain. The man I'm talking about in this chapter, Joseph Banks, is also mentioned elsewhere in this book in connection with breadfruit. The story behind breadfruit is so interesting I thought it deserved a whole section to itself. So in this chapter I must avoid repeating myself. Please stop me if I talk about breadfruit!

Luckily there are a lot of other interesting things to say about Joseph Banks. In particular, his time aboard HMS *Endeavour* on a voyage to the South Pacific between 1768 and 1771. This was one of the most important sea journeys in history, which went on to shape the lives, deaths and destinies of millions of people. And this expedition, led by Captain James Cook, is one of the most famous sea journeys in the history of the world. The list of destinations visited sounds like the itinerary of a luxury cruise: the subtropical islands of Madeira, the vibrant city of Rio de Janeiro, the rocky headland of Cape Horn, the Pacific islands that make up New Zealand, and the idyllic island of Tahiti, with its lagoons, black-sand beaches and extinct volcanoes. Finally they reached the east coast of Australia, the first European ship to do so. James named the area Botany Bay, which was established as a colony in 1788, and so began Britain's colonization of Australia.

And all this was not even the main purpose of the trip. The official aim of this epic voyage was to determine the astronomical unit. The what? The Astronomical Unit would be a great name for a band. But it is also the name for the distance between the Earth and the sun. Scientists and astronomers knew that if they could measure this distance, they would then be able to measure other distances in the universe, as well as the size of the entire solar system! Scientists hoped that these calculations would produce more accurate information for navigators who used stars and planets to work out their position at sea. No wonder there was a race among European nations to be the first to calculate the astronomical unit.

Scientists realized that one way of calculating the unit could be to watch the passage of the planet Venus across the surface of the sun, and make calculations based on its size. But the passage of Venus doesn't happen very often. It might not happen in someone's entire lifetime. However, one such passage of Venus was due in June 1769, and it was best seen from Tahiti, an island in the middle of the largest and deepest ocean in the world, the Pacific. And this is why the expedition was planned, with scientists and astronomers among the ninety-four passengers. In fact, the ship was described as a 'floating laboratory'. Imagine the pressure on them – because of

CHAPTER 4

how rare the passage of Venus is, if they missed it, there wouldn't be another chance in a generation!

To add to the pressure on the expedition, James had also been given a secret mission from the king himself, sealed in an envelope marked SECRET (yes, really!). This was to find a vast landmass that was suspected to exist in the South Pacific. For many centuries European geographers and mapmakers had imagined that there was an enormous southern continent or *Terra Australis* that covered the southern part of the globe. This was not because they'd ever visited, but because they believed that the continents they did know about in the north would have to be balanced out by a vast continent in the south.

This plan had to be kept under wraps, because the race to calculate the astronomical unit was nothing compared to the race to find and colonize a new continent, with all its possible riches. In fact, there was a French ship, captained by one Jean-François de Surville, which was prowling around the South Pacific at the same time, trying to do exactly that. So the race was on! Winning would be like coming first in the 100 metres at the Olympics, being first to step on the moon, and being victorious in an episode of the BBC's *Race Across the World* all combined.

Now, you may be thinking – well done, you haven't

mentioned breadfruit, but you also appear to have forgotten about Joseph Banks! How come he got to go on this high-stakes voyage? Well, one reason was that he paid good money to join it and take his team aboard. He was from a posh family and was very wealthy. He contributed £10,000 towards the trip (nearly £1.5 million in today's money). In comparison, King George III only gave £4,000! It was a bit like when rich people today pay vast amounts to join a journey into space or down to the bottom of the ocean to see the wreck of the *Titanic* (a luxury ship that sank in 1912).

But Joseph was more than just a rich man with a taste for adventure. He was obsessed with science and botany, which is the word given to the scientific study of plants. Encouraged by his mother, he had been fascinated by nature since he was a child. Here's a strange story for you: at the time, toads were considered by many to be evil creatures that gave you warts. His mother told him they were, in fact, harmless, and so the mischievous young Joseph enjoyed picking up toads and rubbing them on his face to shock people. Fun!

As he got older, Joseph got more serious about botany. He started spending less time rubbing toads on his face and more time learning about insects and plants. And even though he was studying at the University of

CHAPTER 4

Oxford, he also paid for his own botany tutor. (You might not consider hiring a tutor for relaxation yourself, but that was his idea of a good time! They didn't have PlayStations in those days.) Then, when his father died and he inherited a huge amount of money, he started travelling. And when he heard about the *Endeavour* expedition, he offered to fund it and to come along for the ride. And thanks to his expert knowledge the twenty-five-year-old Joseph was a valuable crew member. He also took two other brilliant botanists with him: Daniel Solander and Herman Spöring.

As well as observing Venus, crew members on the expedition were expected to collect samples and record the plants and wildlife they encountered in these unknown new lands. Botany was incredibly important at this time, because much of the success of Britain's empire was based on products that come from plants, such as cotton, spices and wood. Another example of an important plant, very connected to Joseph, is breadf–

Phew, stopped myself in time!

The *Endeavour* left Plymouth on 26 August 1768. Alongside Joseph and his fellow scientists, the ninety-four people on board included artists to record the trip (there was no photography in those days, of course), a cook and a surgeon, for any accidents and illnesses. And sadly

CHAPTER 4

there were several deaths on the first leg of the journey. At Rio de Janeiro in Brazil a seaman called Peter Flower fell overboard and drowned. At Tierra del Fuego, the very cold southernmost tip of South America, Joseph and Daniel decided to go ashore with a small party to collect plants. They got caught in a snowstorm, and two Black servants, Thomas Richmond and George Dorlton, froze to death.

The *Endeavour* had a wide variety of inhabitants. The youngest person on board was the eleven-year-old Nicholas Young (if you think this is a suitable name, so did his shipmates – they called him Young Nick!), who was a servant to the ship's surgeon. Just think – as a modern eleven-year-old, you might be sorting out your school uniform ahead of the start of Year Seven and trying to work out how to join Chess Club. Back then they might have been setting off for a three-year adventure on the high seas!

Also on board were a farm's worth of animals: sheep, cattle, ducks, a goat, a boar, a sow and her piglets, and the ship's dogs and cats. The livestock were on board to supply fresh meat and eggs. The goat was there to provide milk. She had just returned from a voyage around the world on a ship called the *Dolphin* (1766–68), and when she survived her second trip, she became famous as the Well-Travelled Goat!

It must have been cosy below deck to put it mildly, as

the *Endeavour* was really quite small. The ship itself no longer exists, as she sank in 1778, but an exact replica of her has been built. If you want to get an idea of what it was like to live on board, you can go to the website of the Australian National Maritime Museum, where you can take a virtual tour. The best room on the ship, the Great Cabin, was usually reserved for the captain, but on this voyage VIPs like Joseph and the other scientists got to hang out there too. Lesser crew members – and certainly a lowly servant like Nicholas Young – would have slept in a hammock on a crowded deck with no privacy.

Can you imagine how thrilling – and nerve-racking – an expedition like this must have been? The crew were sailing off into the great unknown, not knowing when they would return. Or if they would return! There was always the danger of death on a voyage – from diseases, accidents, fights and shipwrecks – and this expedition was particularly risky. There were no maps to follow, and no way of knowing what lay in store.

One seafaring tradition that both Joseph and the young Nicholas would have had to endure was 'crossing the line'. This was a ceremony for sailors who were crossing the equator for the first time (the imaginary line round the Earth that marks the middle of the planet) and involved being ducked in a vat of water. If you're

CHAPTER 4

imagining something like bobbing for apples, think again: this was much more brutal. Your legs were tied to a piece of wood, you were then lifted into the air by a machine and dropped into water three times. Some people could drown or get squished by the machine. It was not just humans who endured it, but the cats and dogs as well! (It sounds like the piglets were spared.)

After stops in Madeira, Rio and Cape Horn, in April 1769, the *Endeavour* reached Tahiti. Yes, they got there in time to observe the passage of Venus – phew! They also picked up the Tahitian navigator, mapmaker and priest Tupaia, who would help them on their continuing journey, acting as an interpreter, a guide and a kind of diplomat. While they were there, Joseph also encountered a native plant that he thought had real potential for use in the British Empire. The name begins with 'b' and rhymes with dead fruit. See page 76 for more details!

So that was the first official part of the mission out of the way. Now for the secret part: trying to beat the French to claim this rumoured southern continent.

First, the *Endeavour* reached what is now New Zealand. As the ship approached the east coast of the country, James offered a gallon of rum to whoever sighted land first and he promised to name somewhere after them. Nicholas Young won! He got the gallon of rum and had a headland named after him: Young Nick's Head. The original Māori name for the headland is Te Kurī a Pāoa.

While charting the coastline, Cook and his crew had both peaceful interactions and violent skirmishes with the people living there. Indigenous people had inhabited this part of the world for centuries – specifically, there were Aboriginal and Torres Strait Islander peoples of Australia and the Māori peoples of Aotearoa New Zealand. They were treated with extreme cruelty by the Europeans, who refused to see them as fellow human beings. As the colonization of New Zealand and Australia continued, they suffered terrible violence, injustice and disease.

After six months mapping the New Zealand coastline, James Cook claimed the territory for the British crown. They then continued the voyage, and eventually reached the east coast of Australia in April 1770, landing close to what is now the state capital of New South Wales, Sydney. This was not the magic and massive so-called *Terra Australis*, the southern continent of their dream, James decided. It

CHAPTER 4

was completely different to what they had imagined! But he thought it was a pretty interesting place anyway.

The place they landed in already had a name: the Gweagal people from the Dharawal Nation called it Kamay. But as I explained on pages 41–2, British colonists liked to rename things, and James christened their landing place Stingray Harbour – presumably, it was full of those beautiful, wafting flat sea creatures. But after Joseph collected a huge number of plants there, it was renamed Botany Bay. As well as the plants, Joseph was excited by the sighting of a new creature called a kangaroo, now seen as Australia's most famous animal. One of the ship's dogs, a greyhound, tried to outrun this springy new creature but lost!

As part of the briefing for his top-secret mission, James had been instructed by the British government to claim new land only if no one was living there. Or if people did live there already, the government said that he needed their consent. Although there were people already living in Australia, he did not get their permission before he claimed the land for Britain. His decision is highly controversial to this day, as James's voyage was ultimately a tragic one. It eventually resulted in the deaths of huge numbers of Aboriginal and Torres Strait Islander peoples, as the British violently stole their land and introduced new diseases. But this didn't begin until nearly twenty years later.

After four months, the *Endeavour* began her long journey home, stopping off at Batavia (now known as Jakarta), in the Dutch West Indies. This was a mistake, as all but ten of the people on board fell ill with malaria (a serious disease that is spread through mosquitoes) and dysentery (a dangerous infection that leads to a very upset stomach), including Joseph, and many died.

Finally, in July 1771, the ship arrived back in Britain. Although they hadn't found any evidence of the fabled southern continent, this did not stop the press from reporting that they had (fake news is nothing new!). The expedition was seen as a huge success in Britain; they had observed the passage of Venus, mapped much of the South Pacific, claimed several new territories for the British and, of course, brought home a lot of plant samples – 30,000 of them! James became a national hero and went on to make two more voyages to the Pacific.

As for the now fourteen-year-old Nicholas Young, he went back to school and started preparing for his mock GCSEs. Joke! We don't know what happened to Nicholas Young, but I hope he got some glory by being able to tell his friends about the passage of Venus.

And what happened to Joseph Banks? Well, he became as famous as a botanist can be. He joined the Royal Society, a prestigious scientific institution (later he would

CHAPTER 4

become its president), helped to establish London's famous botanical gardens at Kew and continued to use his wealth and expertise to advance the empire.

As a result of Joseph's activities, eighteen years after the *Endeavour* first reached Botany Bay, eleven ships (known as the First Fleet) headed back out there. The British had a problem with overcrowded prisons, and they decided that Botany Bay would be a suitable site to create a colony for criminals. With more than 1,400 convicts, settlers, officers and sailors on board, they arrived on 26 January 1788. This was the start of the British colonization of Australia. For Aboriginal and Torres Strait Islander peoples the arrival of the First Fleet was an invasion, a terrible loss of land, accompanied by violence and disease. Within fourteen months of the First Fleet's arrival, a vast number of Aboriginal peoples had died of smallpox. In Australia today 26 January is known as Australia Day and is celebrated as a public holiday. But for many it is a day of sorrow, sometimes called 'Invasion Day'.

Joseph Banks also offered a reward to anyone successful in transporting 1,000 breadfruit plants from Tahiti to the West Indies, so they could be grown there to feed enslaved people on plantations. Yes, I know – I mentioned the B-word. But, look, we're almost at the end!

So how should we think about the *Endeavour*

voyage? In my favourite phrase, it's complicated. On one hand, the expedition advanced scientific knowledge of the ocean, the solar system and the natural world. Joseph Banks and James Cook were mostly interested in discovery and sharing knowledge, and perhaps the fame that would give them. But their journey led to a darker, more harmful phase of colonization, which resulted in a great deal of destruction for Indigenous communities. The pain is still felt today, but modern-day Aboriginal and Torres Strait Islander peoples are also taking on these negative legacies by revitalizing their languages, reviving ancient ways of managing land and sharing their cultural knowledge through arts and books.

Banks and Cook often described many parts of this region as barely inhabited, but of course that was not the case. If you have visited the website of the Australian National Maritime Museum to look at the *Endeavour* replica, you will have seen a message flash up paying respects to the region's First Peoples. Such statements, called Acknowledgement of Country, are part of Australia's efforts to address its colonial past – which all started with HMS *Endeavour* dropping anchor at Botany Bay. That £10,000 which Joseph Banks gave to fund the journey ultimately led to Aboriginal, Torres Strait Islander and Māori peoples paying a much higher price.

BREADFRUIT

You may know about breadfruit, especially if you are of Jamaican or other Caribbean heritage. For those who don't - it grows on trees and looks a bit like a knobbly football-sized lime with pale flesh inside. Despite its name, it is used like a vegetable, roasted and sliced like a potato. It tastes quite sweet and bland, has a chewy texture and a smell when cooked that is similar to - you've guessed it - bread! This interesting fruit has a *very* interesting history. I mean, what other fruits can claim to be both a legacy of empire and slavery *and* a symbol of resistance to empire and slavery?

Let me explain. As we just learned in the last chapter, in 1768, James Cook sailed to the South Pacific on board HMS *Endeavour* alongside Joseph Banks, a botanist. While in Tahiti, Joseph was introduced to a local plant called breadfruit. He soon realized its potential as a food crop, not least because it was easy to grow in large quantities, bearing fruit three times a year.

You see, at that time Britain was heavily involved in the transatlantic slave trade. Slave labour in the Caribbean produced lots of valuable sugar for the people who owned enslaved people, but it meant that they also had a lot of enslaved people to feed. Also, this part of the world relied on food supplies from nearby North America. But with growing unrest between Americans and their British rulers, trade was sometimes unreliable and there were growing concerns about food shortages.

The British could have allowed enslaved people to grow more of their own food, but they worried this might lead them to work less, to become less reliant on the British for supplies and eventually lead to uprisings. Joseph thought that growing breadfruit was the answer. He decided to transport breadfruit plants from Tahiti to the Caribbean islands St Vincent and Jamaica.

CHAPTER 4

The first attempt was in 1787 on HMS *Bounty*, which was fitted with a specially made greenhouse for the plants. Unfortunately the voyage never reached its destination, as the crew staged a rebellion - a story that has inspired no fewer than five films! There was another attempt, and by the end of 1793 the British had planted nearly 700 breadfruit trees in the Caribbean, ready to produce food for the plantations. The only problem? The enslaved workers refused to eat breadfruit! They said it was only fit for feeding pigs.

Fast-forward to today, and as I mentioned, breadfruit has become part of the Caribbean diet. How and why did this happen if their ancestors among the enslaved never took to breadfruit? Some historians think that when the enslaved people refused to eat it back then, it wasn't really about it tasting bad, it was more about resisting those awful slave owners. This is why breadfruit is seen by some as a symbol of resistance to slavery.

CHAPTER 5

Searching for the Source of the Nile: David Livingstone, 1813–73

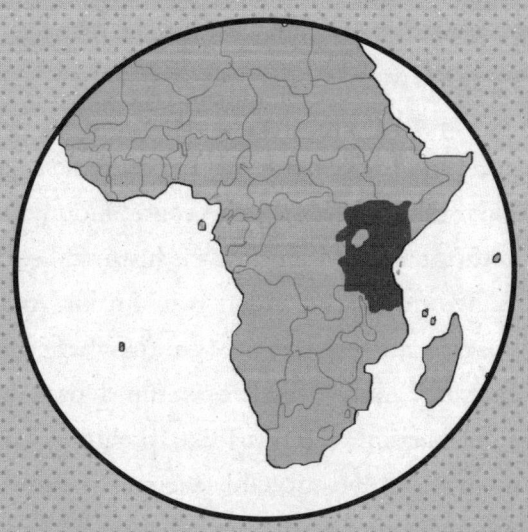

CHAPTER 5

If you want to go down in history as a great explorer, it really helps to come up with an epic quote. You know, the kind that you can imagine a gravelly-voiced man saying in a film trailer or as an inspirational slogan on TikTok. Like 'One small step for man, one giant leap for mankind' (Neil Armstrong, the first man on the moon) or 'It is not the mountain we conquer, but ourselves' (Edmund Hillary, the first man to reach the top of Everest). Well, Dr David Livingstone was pretty good at these.

The Victorian explorer travelled across Africa, attempting to spread Christianity, to stamp out the slave trade, to reach parts of the continent that no European had before, and to encounter the source of the great River Nile. This was one of the last geographic mysteries to solve in the nineteenth century, the historical equivalent of working out where you left your PE kit. Among his quotes are: 'I am prepared to go anywhere, provided it be forward', and 'I shall open up a path into the interior, or perish!' (Sayings I like to employ whenever I end up in Ikea.) But probably the most famous saying associated with him wasn't actually said by him. It was said *to* him, by a man who had travelled all the way from the West to find him, when he was assumed lost in Africa or even dead.

SOURCE OF THE NILE: DAVID LIVINGSTONE, 1813–73

But before we get on to that famous quote, let's first find out what the guy actually did. David Livingstone was born in Scotland in 1813 into a poor family. *Really* poor. Think seven children sharing one single room! At the age of ten he was put to work in a cotton mill, crawling under dangerous machines to fix them, from 6 a.m. to 8 p.m., and *then* he'd do his homework. Maybe a day at school with double maths after lunch doesn't seem quite so torturous now?

As well as being poor and hard-working, his family were also very religious, and when David was twenty-one, he decided to become a *missionary*, travelling overseas to spread Christianity. In preparation, he studied Greek, theology and medicine, and then, in 1840, he set sail for Cape Town. As soon as he set foot in Africa, he fell in love with the continent, and would remain there for most of his life.

His first few years were spent travelling around South Africa and having adventures fit for storybooks. One of these adventures was in 1843 in Mabotsa, when he was asked to help shoot a lion that was terrorizing villagers. He took a shot but didn't kill the animal and the lion was furious (as you would be in its position). It clamped David's arm between its teeth and shook him 'as a terrier dog does a rat'. The lion also attacked and injured

CHAPTER 5

local people, including Mebalwe Molehabangwe, who drew the lion's attention away from David. David was badly injured but survived and later wrote in a letter to his future father-in-law that 'the lions here are very numerous and very troublesome'. Which seems like an understatement. David was not an excitable fellow.

He is said to have had another adventure when trekking through the jungle with a companion. The story goes that he spotted some stones on the ground, picked them up and threw them away. When asked why he had done that, he said that they were diamonds, and he didn't want lots of fortune hunters rushing to the place, which was something that was happening more and more often. Perhaps this diamond story isn't quite as thrilling as the lion one, and it's a story that has been repeated many times without there being a huge amount of evidence for it having happened. But it might be an illustration of the fact that in David's time some people cared more about exploring a new place, rather than just *exploiting* it. That came later. (And if it *did* happen, it also shows once again that it took a lot to excite David – I'd be thrilled to find diamonds on a walk!)

Oh, and I almost forgot – David also trekked across the Kalahari Desert on another trip, and he personally freed eighty-four enslaved people from a slave trader!

SOURCE OF THE NILE: DAVID LIVINGSTONE, 1813-73

He came across the band of enslavers when he was travelling as part of an armed group of explorers and missionaries. Together the group took the decision to free the captives. This was achieved with little violence, but a week later there was a fight between members of the enslaving tribe and the Europeans. The Europeans killed six Africans and burned down their village. Among the eighty-four people freed were two boys, Chuma and Wakotani. David arranged for them to be educated at a Christian school in India, and they later joined him on his expeditions in Africa.

Amid all this adventure, David found time to get married to the daughter of a fellow missionary and have six children. But when his young daughter died, he decided to send his family back to Britain, because life on these travels was proving dangerous. It was then that he really ramped up his exploration, announcing his plans to journey into the heart of the African continent, where no European had explored before.

Yes, this was the time for one of his famous sayings. In this case: 'I shall open up a path into the interior, or perish!' His mission was to find a route from the centre of the continent to the coast. This, he hoped, would help end the East African slave trade, through what he called 'Christianity and commerce'. In other words, he wanted to make it easier for local people to trade other products, such as ivory, as an alternative to slave trading. And he believed that by spreading Christianity, he would be spreading 'civilized' values.

Another quick reminder that there were different kinds of slavery and slave trades around the world at this time in history. There was the transatlantic slave trade, which we learned about in Chapter 3, that was controlled by Europeans. There was the slave trade in Central Asia, which we will read about in Chapter 6. And then there was the East African slave trade, which was controlled by traders usually from Africa or Middle Eastern countries.

OK, back to the 'path into the interior, or perish!' story. So David came across the Zambezi River, which was 1,000 miles long and led to the ocean, and was everything he was looking for. As a bonus, he was also taken by his local guides to a spectacular vast waterfall, at a spot now on the border of Zambia and Zimbabwe. The locals called it Mosi-oa-Tunya, or 'the Smoke that Thunders'. David was the first white person to see it, and, as explorers of that time often did, he named it after the British queen: *Victoria Falls*. I think we can agree that David's way with words let him down here. 'The Smoke that Thunders' is a much better name!

During this trip, David crossed Africa from coast to coast but failed to find the source of the Zambezi River. However, he did not give up. In fact, he decided – in the words of a slogan from way before your time, from my youth in the 1980s and 1990s – to 'Go big or go home'! He decided instead to find the source of the Nile, which was then considered the longest river in the world.*

Finding the source of this river was an almost mythical quest for explorers, like discovering a new planet today or finding out where lost socks go. Starting with the ancient Romans, many had tried and failed. At the time David was roaming around the continent, a rival British explorer called John Hanning Speke claimed to have found it at Lake Victoria (see, I told you they all did the naming-after-the-queen thing). But yet another explorer, Richard Burton, claimed this wasn't true. The two men were going to have a public debate on the subject, but then, on the morning of the debate, John tragically died while out hunting.

So, with people still questioning where the source of the Nile was, David decided to take up the challenge of finding it. If he succeeded, he thought, he would

---

* People still argue about this, but some research suggests the Amazon might be slightly longer.

CHAPTER 5

become even more famous and this would strengthen his campaign for the abolition of the slave trade. In 1866, he and a group of local guides and followers set off from Zanzibar. David was accompanied by more than thirty porters, guides and soldiers, including the previously enslaved Chuma and Wakotani. To carry supplies and luggage, they had a strange combination of animals: six camels, three buffaloes (and a calf), four donkeys and six mules. David also took along his pet poodle!

The first part of the journey was through thick rainforest, full of biting, disease-carrying insects called tsetse flies. They made their way along the banks of rivers, climbed mountains and crossed unhealthy marshes. The journey was so difficult that his attendants argued and started to desert him. The animals fell ill and died. David struggled with his health, suffering from bouts of fever and even collapsing at times.

On returning to Zanzibar without their leader, the deserters claimed that David had been killed by a tribe, as they didn't want to get into trouble for leaving him. It was only several months later that this claim was discovered to be untrue. His death might have been fake news, but David was indeed in bad health. Nonetheless, he pressed on. Remember: 'I am prepared to go anywhere, provided it be forward!'

CHAPTER 5

Spoiler alert – he didn't find the source of the Nile. But he did get further west in central Africa than any European had before, reaching Nyangwe, on the Congo River.

Back in Britain and America, the newspapers and authorities hadn't heard from David for several years, and were wondering what had happened to him. A journalist from the *New York Herald*, Henry Stanley, was sent to Africa to track him down. If this seems surprising, then remember that explorers were the rock stars of the Victorian era. So imagine if Harry Styles or Taylor Swift went missing when on tour – if Harry Styles or Taylor Swift had a walrus moustache and a wonky arm from that lion attack! Amazingly, considering there was no Google Maps back then, in the autumn of 1871 Henry managed to locate David. He was at Lake Tanganyika, in the country we know today as Tanzania, and was quite unwell.

And finally it's time for David's best-known-slogan-even-though-he-didn't-actually-say-it! 'Dr Livingstone, I presume?' said Henry, greeting the great explorer.

Henry gave David medicine to help him recover and they spent four months together. When it was time for Henry to return home, he asked David to come with him but David refused. He was still determined to find the source of the Nile. However, by this point he was so weak he had to be carried around in a hammock. He wrote in a letter, with his typical lack of drama: 'It is not all pleasure, this exploration.' Another saying that can be useful in Ikea. This classic Victorian understatement would be Dr Livingstone's last memorable quote. In May 1873, in a village in what is now northern Zambia, he was discovered dead, kneeling by his bed, hands together as if praying.

His heart and main organs were removed and buried nearby, and his remains embalmed – a process in which chemicals are used to preserve a dead body. The man who embalmed him, James Chuma, was one of the enslaved people David had freed years before and he had been at the explorer's side ever since. James and a team of men who had worked with David then carried the body on a sixty-three-day journey to the Atlantic coast. It was then sailed back to England, where David was given a hero's funeral at Westminster Abbey in London.

In written accounts of his life and death, what David actually died from is often glossed over. That's because part of what caused his suffering was considered embarrassing. The poor man had severe haemorrhoids, or piles, which are painful swollen veins in your bottom. Although these are very common and can be easily treated

CHAPTER 5

nowadays, it's likely that this is what eventually killed him, perhaps in combination with illnesses like dysentery and malaria. I'm telling you not because I enjoy embarrassing dead explorers or because I think things to do with bottoms are funny (not at all!), but because it's a reminder that great heroes, the Harry Styles of their day, are also just people with bottoms, like the rest of us.

David's legacy is sometimes glossed over too. He had gone to Africa to try to convert African people to Christianity and to grow British influence. He might have been trying to increase trade in Africa and get rid of the slave trade, but this was also a way of bringing Africa under British control, and helping British businesses make money. And David's exploration of Africa helped pave the way for the colonization of the continent. His maps were useful for the colonizers who followed. His ideas about commerce, Christianity, civilization (known as the three Cs) and the abolition of the slave trade were used to justify the activities of European powers in Africa. Not long after he died came the 'Scramble for Africa', when a number of European powers, including Britain, rushed to colonize African countries and seize the land for its natural resources, such as oil, ivory and rubber.

The colonizers took a map of the continent and split it

up, drawing borders in new places (have you ever noticed that the map of Africa is full of loads of weird straight lines?). They didn't think at all about any of the people or communities who had lived there for many centuries. A lot of the time they didn't really know or care that the people here were all different, with their own traditions, beliefs and ways of living life. Controlling Africa also made it easier to control trade routes to colonies in India and the rest of the world.

Oh yes, and those diamonds, which David might or might not have stumbled across. South Africa's secret treasure didn't stay secret for long. Around the time of David's death, a man called Cecil Rhodes moved out there and started digging for diamonds. His company, De Beers, would go on to produce ninety per cent of the world's diamonds. (And De Beers later came up with its own famous slogan: 'A diamond is forever'.)

Not satisfied with that, Cecil, who had some very racist views, went on to seize control of the areas of Africa we now call Zimbabwe and Zambia, and the new colony was eventually named Rhodesia after him by white settlers. In charge of the London-based British South Africa Company, which was set up to benefit British business interests in that part of the world, Cecil Rhodes seized land from African people and made them work on it, paying them next to nothing to build his fortune. He helped to spread British power over Africa to make himself rich – and the work done by people like David Livingstone helped him.

We need to remember that alongside every famous white explorer at this time, there were millions of people who had already 'discovered' the land, whose families had lived there for generations. Also, these explorers were aided by local helpers, unsung heroes with expert knowledge, without whom the explorers could not have achieved what they did. Many of these explorers didn't care about their guides, but some were even worse to them. One, Halford Mackinder, is even believed to have shot eight of his guides when trying to climb Mount Kenya.

PS: In case you were thinking of heading off on an expedition to find the source of the Nile yourself, I must tell you that it has since been confirmed that John Hanning Speke was correct. The source of the longest river in Africa is indeed Lake Victoria, the largest lake in Africa.

THE ROYAL FAMILY

Strictly speaking the British royal family did not come about as a result of the British Empire. This country has had monarchs going far, far further back than the start of empire, which properly began when Queen Elizabeth I was in charge. And those who paid attention in history lessons will know that there were many monarchs before Elizabeth I. Such as her not-so-dear father Henry VIII. You know, the one with all the wives. And all those other Henrys. And Edwards. Going all the way back to poor forgotten Athelstan, the first king of England, who was crowned about 1,100 years ago.

Many of the things we associate with the royals, however, are a legacy of the empire. The grand surroundings of Buckingham Palace for starters. The modern layout, the setting for so many ceremonies and events, was designed at the height of the British Empire in the early

CHAPTER 5

twentieth century to make London look like a grand imperial city. And the memorial to Queen Victoria, which stands opposite the palace, is packed with references to the British Empire. On the top are two eagles that symbolize the empire. Under the statue of Queen Victoria are the Latin words 'ced*Regina Imperatrix*', which means 'Queen Empress', a reference to the fact that she was named the empress of India.

There was another royal palace in London called Whitehall Palace, which is now gone. This was where British royals held weekly board meetings for the Royal African Company. This British trading company was responsible for sending thousands of enslaved African women, men and children to the Americas, and made money for the royals. Some historians have claimed that there was a horrific practice whereby the Africans delivered to Barbados by this company had the initials 'DY' burned and branded into their skin, representing the Duke of York, or 'RACE', representing the Royal Africa Company of England.

And then there are the Crown Jewels, many of which have direct links with the British Empire. Most controversial is the vast Koh-i-Noor diamond, which many people believe was taken unfairly from India and should be given back. (I've written more about the Crown Jewels in Chapter 10.) And inside the royal palaces are countless other objects and materials gifted by – or taken from – Britain's colonies, ranging from precious artefacts to ivory from elephants and rhinos, and furs from wild animals slaughtered for sport overseas.

CHAPTER 5

Today royal attitudes towards slavery, Empire and the killing of rare animals have shifted. William IV, who defended slavery, was on the throne until 1837, when his niece Victoria succeeded him. Only three years later, her husband, Prince Albert, was speaking out about the evils of the slave trade. More recently Prince William has said that he wants to destroy all items made from ivory in the royal households, calling them 'a symbol of destruction'. This hasn't happened yet, and, in fact, Queen Camilla used an ivory sceptre during King Charles's coronation in 2023. However, she chose *not* to wear a crown featuring the Koh-i-Noor diamond. Slow progress is better than no progress.

CHAPTER 6

The Spy Missions of Arthur Conolly, 1829–41

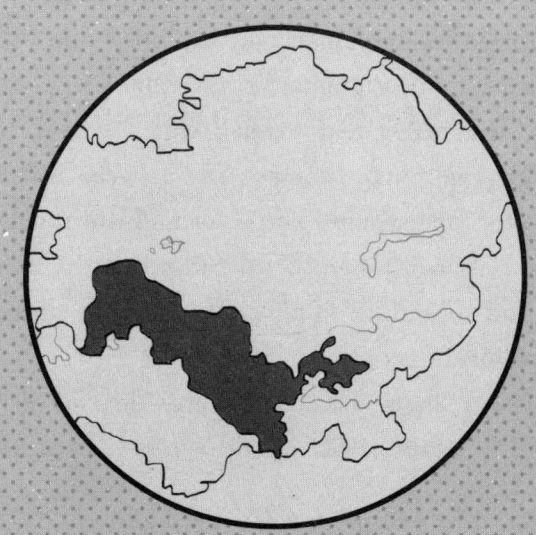

CHAPTER 6

Wouldn't it be cool to coin a phrase? By that I mean coming up with a way of describing something that catches on and becomes a thing. I really should resist giving current examples, because by the time this book is published they'll have aged like milk and make me seem even older than I already am. But here goes. Wouldn't it have been cool to come up with 'skibidi' or 'rizzler' or 'fanum tax'?

Sorry, sorry – I can see you cringing from here. I'll stick to what I do know and tell you about Arthur Conolly, a Victorian military man and explorer, who came up with an extremely popular phrase 200 years ago. The phrase was 'the Great Game', which would become the nickname for the competition between Britain and Russia for influence in Central Asia.* Unfortunately the phrase only really took off decades later, after he had died, and so Arthur didn't get to have the pleasure of hearing lots of people say it.

This is a shame, because towards the end of his life especially, Arthur needed all the comfort and pleasure he

---

* This was a typically imperial phrase, making it sound like a bit of fun, like an exciting round of Monopoly or a jolly good cricket match. But this 'game' often involved lots of killing, and almost certainly didn't feel much like fun for many of the people involved, whose homelands were being invaded by foreign countries.

could get. You see, poor Arthur had a truly awful end – pretty much the worst one imaginable. In fact, it was the terribleness of his death that he first became famous for. But we'll come to all that.

Arthur's life started off pretty normally. He was born in London in 1807, the third of six sons, and attended Rugby School. As well as being a famous public school, Rugby is where a certain popular ball game was invented. I'll leave it to you to work out which one.

If you're wondering whether there's a connection between the phrase 'the Great Game' and the games that the men of the time played at school, then clever you! As we saw on page 59, at the time it was commonly thought that the character traits needed for building an empire – being fair, strong and a good team player – were the same traits found on school cricket, football and rugby pitches. Also, some people thought that the best students for the job were those who were not too clever or too much of a swot – the empire needed men who could take orders and carry them out without thinking too much or asking too many questions!

As it happens, Arthur himself was a shy and sensitive boy, and he hated Rugby School. At the age of fifteen, he left and joined the British army, serving in Bengal in India. A few years later, he got sick and returned home,

CHAPTER 6

but he now had a taste for adventure, and in his early twenties he returned to Asia by travelling across Europe and beyond. Most people travelled directly by sea, but travelling there overland turned out to be so exciting that he wrote a successful book about it, which was called *A Journey to Northern India*. Nowadays a journey to northern India from the UK might involve a train to the airport followed by a nine-hour flight to Delhi – roughly enough time to binge-watch one season of *SpongeBob*. Back then it took Arthur a year and a half, and involved travelling through France and Germany before sailing over to Russia and entering Central Asia.

The region had some lawless and hostile areas, so to avoid falling into trouble, Arthur often travelled in disguise as a local, calling himself Khan Ali, as a play on his surname (geddit? Say it out loud if you don't). One particularly risky part of his trip was his attempt to enter Persia (now Iran) in disguise as a local merchant on a camel. With his Indian companion, Karamat Ali, Arthur joined a group of travellers to cross the desert. He draped himself in scarves, furs and shawls, and bought sacks of spices as props. Some days into their journey, a party of four horsemen galloped up, offering the travellers protection. The horsemen were not convinced by Arthur's disguise and thought he was a Russian spy.

Instead of protecting the travellers, the horsemen ended up robbing them. After a few days' wandering in the desert, some merchants took pity on Arthur and Karamat Ali and escorted them back to the city. They were saved from potentially being killed or sold into slavery. Arthur then wisely chose a different route, through Persia and Afghanistan, before finally making it to India.

Around this time, tensions were rising between Britain and the Russian Empire. Russia controlled some of Central Asia and wanted to control even more, claiming that this was necessary in order to stamp out slavery in the region. The slavery in Central Asia was not the same as transatlantic slavery, which we learned about in Chapter 3. By the period we are talking about here, around 1838, the British were no longer involved in the transatlantic slave trade and had abolished slavery in most of their colonies. But slavery occurred elsewhere on a smaller scale, including in the Central Asian countries we now call Uzbekistan and Turkmenistan. Most of the slaves there were Muslims from Persia, but a small number of Russians were also captured, and this was the reason Russia said it needed control of the region. The Russian Empire's takeover of Central Asia made the British nervous, because it meant there was suddenly a rival dangerously close to Britain's prize colony, India.

CHAPTER 6

Step forward Arthur, who was now working as an intelligence officer, or spy, in Calcutta, within the East India Company's political department. He suggested that the British offer to talk to the leaders of the states in Central Asia, and try to reach an agreement with them to stop enslaving Russians and Persians. This would remove Russia's excuse to invade and could increase British influence there. Arthur's bosses agreed.

Arthur was given another task while he was in the region: to negotiate the release of a British hostage being held by the ruler of the Emirate of Bukhara. This is a state that existed from 1785 to 1920 in what is now Uzbekistan, Tajikistan, Turkmenistan and Kazakhstan. The man was called Colonel Charles Stoddart, and he had been jailed while on a diplomatic mission to Bukhara. He had been sent to deliver a letter to the leader, or emir, stating that the British had no intention of invading his country. So Charles had gone to Bukhara in peace.

In that case, why had he been imprisoned? Had he murdered someone? Stolen stuff? No. He had just been a bit of a wally and had forgotten to take the leader of Bukhara a present. Now we all like presents. And we all know the feeling when it's our birthday or Christmas and a visitor arrives who we're expecting a present from – Uncle Ravi, say, or your mum's best friend – and they don't deliver. You were hoping for the new Rick Riordan book, or a friendship-bracelet kit or maybe a Roblox gift card. But nothing. You might feel a little bit disappointed. Well, the emir wasn't just a little bit disappointed; he was utterly insulted and murderously furious. That's how the notoriously ruthless leader of Bukhara, Emir Nasrullah Khan – nicknamed 'The Butcher' – felt when, in 1839, Charles turned up to visit empty-handed. Also, the Englishman rode into the city on horseback, rather than entering on foot, which was seen as disrespectful. As a punishment for forgetting his manners, he was thrown into prison. So the next time you get told off for not saying 'please' or 'thank you', be grateful. You got off lightly!

Now, though, Arthur was going to Charles's rescue. He had received a letter from Charles saying that the emir was inviting him there. In November 1841, Arthur arrived in Bukhara. And guess what happened? It was a trap! He too was captured and thrown into Zindon prison, alongside Charles.

Some say the emir was suspicious of Arthur's activities, while the renowned historian Peter Frankopan suggests he was annoyed by foreign powers interfering with his country. The British might have acted like they wanted

CHAPTER 6

to help in this part of Central Asia, but really they were just looking after their own interests.

And when I say he was thrown into prison, I mean a special part of the prison that also had its own nickname – 'the Bug Pit'. Whoever came up with that isn't going to get any prizes for imagination, because that's exactly what it was. A dungeon, dug into the ground, filled with insects. If you're squeamish, I'd advise skipping the next bit. Maybe go and get a snack. I'll give you a shout when it's safe to come back.

For those still here, let's get down to the grisly details about life in the Bug Pit. The hole was about four metres deep, and accessible only by rope. It was squirming with rats, insects and scorpions, and every so often guards topped up the insects and threw in some horse manure as an extra treat. The prisoners were fed but were not allowed any luxuries, such as changing their clothes. They went to the toilet in the pit, to add to the filth.

By the time Arthur arrived in Bukhara, Charles had already been in solitary confinement in the Bug Pit for two years. Two years! Can you even imagine? At least now, with Arthur, Charles had some company. The two men lived together in the pit for many more months. Arthur managed to write a few letters from the dungeon that described the appalling conditions, using the blank

CHAPTER 6

pages of a Christian prayer book. He wrote that they were: 'resolved to wear our English honesty and dignity to the last within all the misery and filth that this monster may try to degrade us with'.

The emir was random as well as ruthless, and occasionally he would order the men's release, giving them hope that their ordeal was at an end, before changing his mind and throwing them back into the Bug Pit again. Finally, in June 1842, they were hauled out of the pit for good.

According to an account, their 'bodies were covered with sores, their hair, beards and clothes alive with lice'. So had the emir decided the Englishmen had suffered enough? Nope. The two were taken to the public square in Bukhara, and charged with spying for the British Empire. And after all those months of horror and torture, Charles was killed. Arthur was told he could live if he became Muslim, but he knew that even if he said yes he would be killed, just as Charles had been. So he said no and he was publicly beheaded.

All of you in the kitchen, you can come back now!

You might think that the moral of this terrible story is to never forget to take a present for your host – especially if they have the nickname 'The Butcher'. And that definitely is worth remembering. But more than that, I think it is a clear illustration of the dangers of the imperial mindset – of believing that one country has the right to enter another country and tell them how to do things.

The story became very well known at the time, and this, along with the emir's nickname (which portrays him as bloodthirsty and vicious), tells us something else about British imperial attitudes at the time. It went down well to portray non-British, non-Christian leaders as crazed or evil, because it made the British Empire look so much better in comparison. There were definitely good leaders in Central Asia who didn't go around throwing foreigners into bug pits or forcing them to convert to Islam. But those stories didn't become so well known, because they didn't strengthen the British case for why they should rule so much of the world.

There is one more story of an Englishman crossing paths with the so-called Butcher of Bukhara – but don't worry, you don't need to go back to the kitchen for this one. In 1845, when Arthur and Charles did not return home, a missionary called Joseph Wolff was sent to look for them. Joseph was a good friend of Arthur's – they had met while in India. And guess what? Yes, the emir threw him into prison too! But perhaps Joseph somehow found his host a good enough present, or perhaps the emir's

CHAPTER 6

heart had softened, or perhaps he was more complicated than the British newspapers of the time believed him to be, because this time the Englishman was released alive. On returning to Britain, Joseph Wolff reported what he had learned about the fate of the two men, and the grisly account was an instant sensation.

The two men became famous, and the author Rudyard Kipling, who also wrote *The Jungle Book*, used them as inspiration for his stories *Kim* and 'The Man Who Would Be King'. Later, Arthur's fame helped popularize his phrase 'the Great Game'. But, of course, all this recognition came too late for the men to enjoy, as they spent their final days in the Bug Pit awaiting their death.

Poor Arthur. His own great game was one he most certainly lost.

NIGERIA

The nation of Nigeria is young. It was only born in 1914. Yes, I know that's over a century ago, but trust me - in country terms that makes it a baby. What's that I hear you say? That there have been people living in that region of West Africa for far, far longer than that? Well, yes, you're right. There is evidence of people living in the land we know as Nigeria many thousands of years ago. What I mean by saying Nigeria is young is that the modern country - with its boundaries and even its name - was invented by the British who colonized it.

Britain had had its eyes on the place we now know as Nigeria since the middle of the nineteenth century.

CHAPTER 6

One of the reasons for this interest was that the land was rich in natural resources, such as rubber and palm oil (which can help make things like margarine and soap). The British also claimed to want to help rid the region of slavery. By this time the international slave trade had been banned but some slavery still continued in West Africa.

To control trade in the region, the British set up the Royal Niger Company, which acted more like a government than a company. The company controlled the area around the River Niger and made local rulers trade only with them. Then, in 1882, they established two zones in the country, the Northern and Southern Protectorates. Being a protectorate means that a place is allowed to govern itself up to a point, but another 'stronger' country - in this case Britain - is ultimately in charge. They are there to 'protect' the 'weaker' country but also to control it.

The British decided to experiment with the protectorates. In the north, a region of ancient

Islamic kingdoms, people were left to continue living their lives largely as they always had done. They were governed by local tribal leaders, and practised traditional religion and medicine. Meanwhile, the British concentrated on the south. They poured money into development, improving roads and building institutions such as schools and churches, and encouraged conversion to Christianity.

You won't be surprised to hear that the two zones quickly became very unequal. At one point, almost all the schools in the country – ninety-five per cent – were in the south. I know what you're thinking. Let's all go back in time and move to the Northern Protectorate! But the inequality of the zones created tensions, as many of the people who lived in the southern areas had been converted to Christianity and were keen on Western education, which helped them get better jobs than people in the north. And this meant the ancient, complex tribal relationships in the region were mucked up by Britain's interference.

CHAPTER 6

Eventually the British decided it was more efficient, and cheaper, to run the area as a single colony. So the northern and southern protectorates were joined together in 1914 - which, as you may recall from the beginning of this section, is when the modern country of Nigeria was born. A British journalist came up with the name!

Finally, in 1960, Nigeria gained its independence, but the problems caused by British rule didn't disappear. Tensions came to a head in 1967 with the brutal Nigerian Civil War (also called the Biafran War), and the wounds are still not fully healed today, with frequent violence between communities.

By the way, Nigeria was not the only nation that came into being because of the British Empire. Many other countries, including Sierra Leone, Singapore, Zimbabwe, Canada and Pakistan, would also not exist in the way they do today, with their particular borders, without British involvement.

CHAPTER 7
The Voyage of *Hesperus* and *Whitby*, 1838

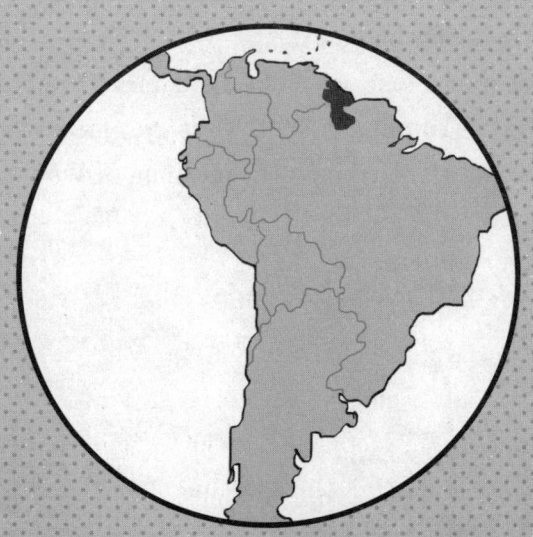

CHAPTER 7

At the risk of sounding like the start of a school assembly, before we begin this chapter I'd like to make an announcement. This chapter is a bit different to the others. The others are about interesting and important journeys of empire and the people who made them. This one is about interesting and important journeys of empire and the *ships* who made them. But the ships were full of passengers and did have names – the *Hesperus* and the *Whitby*. You can think of them as people if you like – people with quite odd names, and people with lots of other people on board . . .

First things first, what do the names 'Hesperus' and 'Whitby' even mean? Well, *Hesperus* means 'evening star' or the planet Venus. The meaning of *Whitby* is less

artistic – its name comes from where the ship was built, which was Whitby in Yorkshire. Some ship owners liked to give their vessels serious and dramatic names like *Endeavour* and *Destiny*. Others chose romantic names from the natural world and space, such as *Hesperus*. And then there were those like the owners of the *Whitby*, who were clearly in a bit of a hurry or had no imagination at all!

So why are we talking about them as a pair? Because on 5 May 1838, they both arrived at the British colony of Guiana in the Caribbean (now called Guyana, and not to be confused with the country of Ghana, in Africa, which was once a British colony named the Gold Coast). On board the two ships were around 396 people who had been hired to work on the sugar plantations. It was a group of people who would go on to change the world.

Now, I know what you might be thinking. Boatloads of labourers bound for back-breaking work on Caribbean plantations sounds an awful lot like transatlantic slavery, which we've talked about elsewhere in this book. But then there's that word 'hired'. Enslaved people weren't hired; they were kidnapped and forced to work for no pay on the plantations. Also, those who are really paying attention (I'm sounding like a school assembly again), might recall

CHAPTER 7

that the transatlantic slave trade was abolished by Britain some years before this. In 1807, the Slave Trade Act made it illegal for Britain to trade in enslaved people. But plantation owners were allowed to continue to use their existing slave labour. The final *emancipation*, or freeing, of enslaved people in Britain's plantation colonies didn't occur until much later.

It's no coincidence that by the time the *Hesperus* and *Whitby* landed in British Guiana in 1838, the once enslaved had been emancipated. The plantation owners wanted to continue producing sugar, but they now needed to replace slave labour. They could, of course, have paid people fairly for the work, including the newly freed enslaved people. But they were used to paying very little for a lot of hard work, and they enjoyed having control, and this is how two boatloads of very, very cheap 'hired' workers ended up there.

The workers came from East India and most were very poor and desperate to earn money. Some had been tricked, and all had signed contracts committing them to work on the plantations for between three and five years for a (small) wage. *Indenture* is another word for this sort of contract, and so they were known as *indentured labourers*. Introducing indentured labour from India to replace slave labour was the idea of a plantation owner called John Gladstone. His son William Gladstone went on to become a very famous politician who was prime minister of Britain a whopping FOUR times, more than anyone else. (Gladstone also holds the record for the oldest UK prime minister in office – he was eighty-four when he finally stepped down in 1894. That makes Joe Biden and Donald Trump seem like spring chickens!)

But all that was in the future. In 1838, John Gladstone wasn't famous for being the father of a record-breaking prime minister but was merely a sugar plantation owner – albeit a very rich one. Now here is something that might blow your mind. After slavery was abolished, the government agreed to pay money (or 'compensation') to those affected. Naturally you'd imagine that this payment would be to the former enslaved people, to acknowledge the horrors they had experienced, right? Wrong! The money was for the slave *owners*, to compensate *them* for the loss of their workers. John Gladstone had owned about 2,500 African enslaved people, and he received £106,769 in compensation when he was forced to let them go. This is equivalent to approximately £9 million today. I know. Beyond belief!

But despite receiving this, Gladstone still wanted to keep making money from his plantations, while paying as little as possible for workers. So he came up with

CHAPTER 7

the idea of using indentured labour from India to keep the sugar production going. The British government agreed to try the plan, and this led to the first arrivals on the *Hesperus* and the *Whitby* in May 1838.

Among the ships' passengers were fourteen women and eleven girls. They had been at sea for 112 days, since leaving the Indian port of Calcutta, during which they had been fed a diet of rice, salt fish and peas. Disease and mistreatment had been rife on board, and eighteen people had died during the journey. The poor hygiene and cramped conditions made cholera (an infection often spread through dirty water) a particular risk – a doctor on board described how the disease could kill a healthy person in just five hours.

Surviving passengers formed strong bonds, as they headed together to an uncertain future. From then on, during their time in British Guiana, they called each other '*jahaji*', which means 'shipmate'. The British had their own name for these workers – 'coolie'. This comes from the word meaning 'hire' or 'wages' in the East Indian language Tamil, and it is now seen as an offensive term.

Typically the people on board carried just one small cloth bundle, often tied to the end of a walking stick, containing all their personal belongings, copies of holy books and perhaps musical instruments. They also took with them seeds and small plants from India, so they could grow the spices and food of their homeland. Spices such as coriander, cumin and turmeric, as well as mango and rice, continue to grow in Guyana today, after being introduced by those indentured workers.

The Indians needed all the home comforts they could get. The life they had signed up to was extremely tough. Labourers were usually housed in shacks where the enslaved had lived previously. These shacks were sometimes furnished with just a rope bed and had clay floors and metal roofs – which made the rooms boiling in the heat. There was often no running water or proper toilets. Not that workers were allowed to spend that much time in their huts; they were out all day working in the fields. Sugar production on plantations involved sowing and harvesting the sugar cane, before removing its juice to boil in enormous vats. All this was done from dawn to dusk under the fierce tropical sun.

Pay was very low, with women paid even less than men, and if a worker did not complete a task in the time they were expected to do it, they would not be paid at all. Rules were very strict, and punishments for those who broke them were severe, ranging from whipping to being thrown into prison.

The workers would occasionally have a glass or

CHAPTER 7

two of rum, a type of alcohol that can be made with sugar cane, and which was invented on what became the British colony of Barbados. But the plantation owners even took advantage of this, by setting up 'grog shops' selling overpriced rum and encouraging workers to spend their tiny wages there. This meant plantation owners often ended up taking back the money they had just paid the workers.

Some workers tried to escape by heading off through the jungle, in the sad hope of somehow walking back to India (thousands of miles away across oceans). The rest had no choice but to work for the years they'd agreed to, after which they could use the very small amount they had saved up to pay for their passage back to India. Or, if they preferred, they could sign up for *another* five years of labour, when they would get a 'free' voyage home.

In short, indentured labour in British Guiana was usually a terrible life, with the workers exploited and abused at every turn. Did those on board the *Hesperus* and the *Whitby* have a clue about what awaited them? Almost certainly not. It's likely that many of them did not even know what was in the contract they signed, because they could not read or write English and had 'signed' with a thumbprint. And even if they did read it, the contract gave little clue as to what life was truly like on the plantations. Many had been lied to.

However, as time passed, word spread about the inhumane ways in which indentured workers were being treated, and a team from the British government was sent to British Guiana to inspect John Gladstone's plantations. They discovered that of the 419 'coolies' who had arrived in May 1838, thirty-eight had died and seventy were sick. After eighteen months, sixty-seven people had died. They were so horrified by what they found that they put a stop to indentured labour for the next five years.

Officials and newspapers in Britain were worried about the scheme. Was indentured labour just a new form of slavery? This is a question that has often been discussed by historians. My view is that although conditions on the plantations were similarly horrific for indentured and enslaved people, there were some important differences between them. One is that the indentured workers had usually agreed to be there. And even though they were not paid a lot for their labour, they were usually paid something. The other difference is that they would be free to leave at some point; their children would not be forced to work on the plantation.

However, the lives of both enslaved people and

indentured workers were incredibly tough, and both suffered cruelty, mistreatment and long gruelling days of work at the hands of the plantation owners. Eventually the scheme was allowed to restart, with new conditions in place to protect the workers. Indentured labour continued in British Guiana and other British colonies, such as Mauritius, Trinidad and Jamaica, until 1920. In total, more than a million Indian workers were recruited to produce sugar, tea, coffee, rubber and cinchona (which helped treat malaria).

When their contracted time was up, the British Guiana workers were free to get a ship back home. However, it may surprise you to hear that most of them stayed. Only 75,000 of the 238,000 who travelled to British Guiana over the years returned to India. I think we can safely guess that this decision to stay was not because it was such fun working on the plantations; in fact, only 6,000 signed up for another five years of work. What is more likely is that once there were more women introduced into the scheme, people started families and settled down, and the colony became their home. By the late 1920s, approximately eighty per cent of the Indians who lived in British Guiana had been born there.

It's a similar story in other British colonies that used Indian labour. Indentured labour is actually one of the reasons there are now so many Indian communities all over the world. These communities are called a *diaspora* – meaning a spread of people who have moved from their original homeland, who have now formed their own distinct culture in a new place. So that is a positive ending to what started out as a pretty miserable story – although an interesting and important one.

And what happened to our odd couple, *Hesperus* and *Whitby*? Well, there were lots of ships called *Hesperus*, so I've found it hard to work out exactly what happened to her. But the *Whitby* continued her journeys around the British Empire; she carried convicts to Australia and settlers to New Zealand. I'd like to think that perhaps, once their miserable work was finished, the two boats, who I will forever see as two people with quite odd names, sailed off together into the sunset.

CHAPTER 7

THE INTERNET

Or, rather, the pattern of cables that makes the internet work.

Yes, I know that doesn't sound quite as mind-blowing as 'the internet' – or as snappy. But, trust me, this story is still pretty extraordinary. It all started with a type of tree called gutta-percha, which grows in South-East Asia. This tree produces a very special sap (the sap is also known as gutta-percha), which is at first flexible but then turns rigid and waterproof at the right temperature. Think of it as a kind of natural plastic.

When Europeans first reached South-East Asia in the late seventeenth century, they found the locals using gutta-percha to make handles for their weapons and walking sticks, and realized its potential. They took it back to Britain, and over time it became widely used for all sorts of things, including to fill tooth cavities. And it is still used for this today. If you've had some serious dentistry, you may have some gutta-percha in your mouth!

But what really excited the British was the discovery that gutta-percha did not conduct electricity. You see, in the 1830s, a man called Samuel Morse (who Morse code is named after – the communication language that allows you to send messages through a sequence of electric pulses) had invented the electric telegraph. This allowed messages to be sent over long distances through copper wires. But it only worked on telegraph lines built on land. Now, though, gutta-percha could be used to coat the copper wires so they could be run underwater.

In 1850, a single copper wire coated with gutta-percha was laid across the English Channel. Unfortunately it was quickly broken by a fisherman's anchor. The experiment was then repeated with a thicker wire, and with some other improvements, and this time it worked.

And international communications were changed forever! Before, it would take weeks, or even months, for a letter to make it from Britain to, say, India. But gutta-percha made sending messages underwater possible, allowing speedy communication and news reporting.

Gutta-percha was used in this way for a century, before being replaced by higher-tech materials. However, today's undersea cables still follow the same routes used back in the nineteenth century. According to the *Sunday Times*, about ninety-seven per cent of the world's internet traffic travels through a million-mile network of wires under the sea. And that is why there is a direct connection between the imperial age and the internet. Gutta-percha played a role in you being able to watch YouTube and play Roblox today.

This story isn't all positive, though. Unfortunately the only way to get gutta-percha sap is to kill the tree. Because the Victorians were so enthusiastic

CHAPTER 7

> about the stuff, it led to millions of trees being destroyed. Today the tree is very rare, and almost extinct in places. So, when you're next watching YouTube, pause for a moment of gratitude for this South-East Asian tree that gave its life to give the world MrBeast.

CHAPTER 8
Adventures in the Middle East: Gertrude Bell, 1868–1926

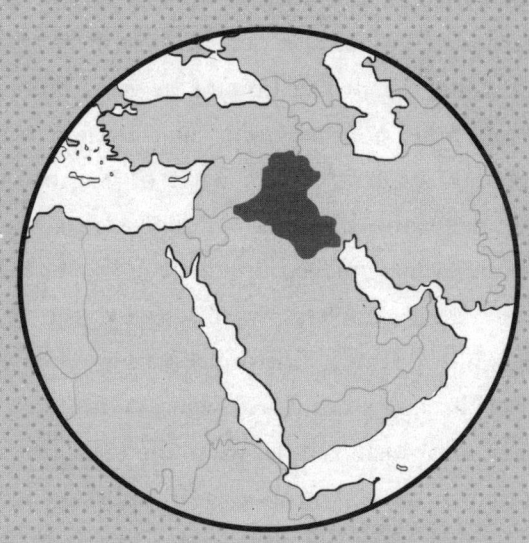

CHAPTER 8

Since you're reading this book, I bet you're a clever person, and that you probably now have a good idea of what *colonization* is. But just a reminder: colonization is when one nation, or power, decides to control another for its own gain. This usually happens with the colonizer entering and occupying the other country. Though this is a bit different to how it works in the made-up universe of *Star Wars*, where the colonization involves the government, known as the Galactic Empire, ruling over an entire galaxy, which contains lots of colonies and territories, and millions of star systems.

In real life, the British Empire, as you'll know from the seven other journeys we have already been on, took charge of territories in parts of North America, Ireland, the Caribbean, Australasia, Africa and Asia. As you might have picked up, the way in which Britain colonized these countries wasn't always the same. In America and Australia, British people settled in the new countries in large numbers, whereas in India small numbers of British people went there to run things, rather than to settle. And, as you already know from this book's introduction, being the well-read person that you are, at its height the British Empire covered a quarter of the Earth's land. But Britain no longer has a vast empire.

So how did the experience of being ruled by the British shape those parts of the world?

It might be helpful here to compare this with what sometimes happens when you go on holiday. You might have been lucky enough to have stayed in a rented holiday home or apartment. At the end of your stay, you (or, let's face it, your adult parents or guardians) hopefully left the place clean and tidy. Beds stripped, floors swept, sinks wiped clean. Rubbish put out in the right bins. Pokémon stickers peeled off the windows. And that's . . . not how colonization worked at all!

Although the situation with each colony was different, the British Empire mostly did *not* leave countries in the same state in which they had been found. And Britain went further than not cleaning up. The British often drastically changed the place they had been colonizing. Going back to that rented holiday home – imagine that, by the time they had left, the colonizers had knocked down walls, changed the rooms around or given the place a new name or number. Or built an extension! Or sold off the garden to a neighbour! Or they might have left the house themselves but let someone else stay there and be in charge. Someone who had never been in charge before.

CHAPTER 8

To make sense of this, it helps to remember that many British people thought that they were doing these countries a big favour by colonizing them, because they thought these countries didn't know how best to look after themselves. And so, while they were in charge, they would try to make changes to 'improve' things, as they saw it. When they left, these changes became their *legacy*. Sometimes they changed the geography, redrawing borders or dividing up land. Sometimes they chose to put someone they liked in charge, rather than letting the citizens vote for their own ruler.

Probably the best-known example of this was in India, where an event known as Partition changed things forever. When the country gained its independence from the British in 1947, it was divided into two separate countries: India (where most people were Hindu) and Pakistan (where most people were Muslim). This division caused huge upset and led to hundreds of thousands of deaths through violence and disease (some say 1 or 2 million), and the problems it created can still be felt today (the two countries have sometimes gone to war).

But now I want to talk to you about Britain's involvement in another region, the Middle East, and the legacy the British Empire left there. This is a part of the world where the British often controlled nations indirectly rather than directly. When Britain ruled directly, this meant Britain had full control over the colony, replacing local leaders with British officials who were there, on the ground, in charge of the territory. When they ruled indirectly, they would use the local leaders and traditional systems of government that were already in place, but really Britain was still in control, making sure that the local leaders acted in Britain's interest by having British 'advisers' working behind the scenes. And one of these cases of indirect rule came about through a quite extraordinary woman named Gertrude Bell.

How extraordinary? Well, she was a spy, and that was actually *not* the most interesting thing about her! Gertrude was born in 1868 to a wealthy family in County Durham, north-east England. Back then women in her position were expected to do two things in life: marry a suitable man and have children. Many Victorians believed that a woman's place was at home, looking after children and cooking and cleaning for the family. The outside world of work and politics was strictly for men.

But Gertrude was a clever young woman and she had other ideas. Firstly she went to study modern history at the University of Oxford, at a time when very few women were students there. Women were not allowed

CHAPTER 8

to use the library, and one of the teachers was so put out at having females in his classes, he ordered them to sit with their backs turned to him! The nineteen-year-old Gertrude got the top marks she needed for a first-class degree, which is like getting a nine in your GCSEs, but she wasn't allowed to actually graduate, because although women could study they weren't allowed degrees from Oxford until 1920. How unfair is that?

After this, her parents thought it was about time she got on with finding a husband. They sent her off to visit her uncle who lived in Persia, in the hope he would introduce her to a suitable man. But instead of falling in love with a man, Gertrude fell in love with travelling through the Middle East. And so began her extraordinary adventures.

In those days women very rarely travelled alone, and the British would not usually travel any further than France or Italy (remember, this was by land only, because air travel wasn't a thing yet). But Gertrude loved what she called 'wild travel', exploring lands that were then part of the Ottoman Empire, such as Syria, Jordan and Palestine.

As its name suggests, the Ottoman Empire was its own empire, not part of the British Empire. The Ottoman Empire covered much of what we now call the Middle

East, and its headquarters was the city of Constantinople, which is modern-day Istanbul in Turkey.

On her travels, Gertrude became fluent in Arabic, Persian, French, German, Italian and Turkish. If Duolingo had been around at the time, she'd have been at the top of her league table! When she wasn't learning all those languages, she liked to climb mountains. But, as you may be gathering by now, when Gertrude did something, she *really* did it. So she became an accomplished mountaineer. In fact, she was the first to reach the summit of seven mountains in the Swiss Alps, including one named after her ('Gertrudspitze'). Her fame increased after she survived for fifty-three hours hanging on to a rope on the previously unclimbed north-east face of the Finsteraarhorn, after she was caught in a terrible storm of snow, hail, thunder and lightning in 1902. She suffered from frostbitten hands and feet but was lucky to escape with her life. And so we can add 'very strong hand grip' to all the other things she excelled at.

Gertrude was also an expert archaeologist. Archaeology is the study of the past through the things people left behind, such as tools, buildings, art and bones. And on an archaeological dig in Turkey, she became friends with the legendary adventurer T. E. Lawrence, aka the camel-riding Lawrence of Arabia.

She wrote a lot of books and reports on a wide range of subjects: her travels, her digging adventures and the political situation in the Middle East during the First World War. She thought that Iraq should be governed indirectly, with local rulers advised by British officials. After the war, she became one of those advisers herself. We'll come back to this shortly, but it's important to know that she was the only woman doing an official job like that in the whole of the British Empire and she was awarded a CBE (standing for 'Commander of the Order of the British Empire'). This honour is still given out to people who have achieved great things today, even though the empire is over.

Oh yes, and I almost forgot – the spy business! Gertrude had been giving information to the British for many years before the First World War. But it was during the war that she was officially hired to work for British intelligence in Cairo, Egypt. Because of her impressive language skills, she could build relationships with a wide range of people and learn a lot about the region and its peoples. During the war, the British depended on her to inform them whether local people would side with Britain or with the enemy. Extraordinary stuff!

But, as I mentioned, the most important bit of Gertrude's life was yet to come. During the First World

CHAPTER 8

War, the Ottoman Empire sided with the Germans against the British. Britain and its ally France came up with a secret plan to divide up the Ottoman Empire's territory if they won, through what was called the Sykes–Picot Agreement (named after the two men who set it up). After Germany and the Ottoman Empire were defeated, the British took control of the regions previously ruled by the Ottomans, including Iraq.

Iraq was especially valuable to the British, because the land contained lots of oil. The war had taught them how important oil was for winning wars, as well as for powering the cars and motorbikes that were becoming part of daily life. Also, it was a fantastic source of money or *revenue*. But they didn't want to actually run the country themselves, as they had done in India and other places. That was expensive, hard and controversial. They believed the Iraqi population would rebel against being directly ruled by Britain; after all, they had just been 'freed' from one empire and might not want to be plunged straight into another one.

That's where Gertrude came in. Knowing her interest and knowledge of the region, the British asked her to help create a new kingdom of Iraq led by their chosen ruler, King Faisal. He was seen as a friend of the British, and they believed he would allow them access to oil.

Gertrude herself wasn't interested in oil or money, but she firmly believed that Britain knew best and that it was her duty to help set up a new Iraq, so she backed Faisal as king and became his adviser.

The legacy of the Sykes–Picot Agreement, and the British presence in the Middle East, has been, to put it politely, *mixed*. Many think this is the root of the religious tensions, unrest and violence in the region, and ultimately what has caused so many years of conflict in places like Israel and Palestine. Also, lots of people blame Britain for the unrest in Iraq throughout the twentieth century, which, in turn, led to war between Iraq and the USA/Britain in the twenty-first century.

But Gertrude also had a legacy. The final years of her life were dedicated to creating an archaeological museum in Iraq, driven by her belief that historical artefacts and treasures should stay in the country they came from. This didn't stop the British from looting Iraqi treasures – go and look in the British Museum for proof! But, thanks to Gertrude, many more artefacts stayed in Iraq than they would have done otherwise.

There's another thing that Gertrude felt very strongly about, but be warned: it's odd! She was a passionate *anti-suffragist*. 'Suffrage' means the right to vote, and in this case, it means women's right to vote. But Gertrude

CHAPTER 8

did not think women should have the right to vote or have their say on political decisions. She described the idea as 'extraordinary and regrettable', and campaigned *against* it.

I know! From our perspective, in the 2020s, it seems completely baffling. The very idea that women were not allowed to vote is weird enough in itself. But even weirder is the idea that a strong and successful woman would be against votes for women. And not just *any* strong and successful woman, but one who had proved herself to be the bravest of the brave and the cleverest of the clever.

To understand, we need to appreciate the attitudes of the time. As mentioned earlier, lots of people believed that men and women were different, and 'designed' for different roles. Society believed that men were strong, logical and smart, and so should be out in the world, dealing with politics, business and money. Women were seen as less intelligent and needing to rely on men. It was said that they were only interested in the home, dealing with cooking, cleaning and looking after children. Even lots of women believed this.

We also need to understand something about Gertrude. She had been born wealthy, and that gave her opportunities that most women did not get. Her privilege gave her access to the 'man's world'. But rather than looking at herself and her achievements and thinking, *I'm proof that all women can do what men do*, she probably thought: *I'm totally different to most other women. I worked hard but they sit at home with their babies, fussing about curtains.*

So while she thought that *she* was able to flourish in a 'man's world', she believed *other* women couldn't, and therefore shouldn't be allowed a say on important matters through voting. In a way, Gertrude's attitude was similar to the wider attitude about the British Empire. Those in favour of the empire believed that Britain was different from, and better than, other countries. This belief is called *exceptionalism*. And because Britain was superior to other countries, they thought, it had a right to rule many of them. This is true of how people saw men and women, and why they thought men should be in charge. Thankfully, since then, these attitudes towards women have changed a lot, and it's far more widely believed that men and women are equal and should therefore be treated equally.

CHAPTER 8

INTERNATIONAL CHARITIES

For a small country Britain has a lot of large international charities working around the world. To name just a few, there's Save the Children, which works to improve the lives of children in more than 100 countries. There's Tearfund, a Christian charity that works to help communities in poverty and disaster-affected areas. And there's Anti-Slavery International, which works to end slavery around the world.

In 2019, some experts published a report that claimed that Britain's collection of international charities was 'among the most remarkable in the world', with significantly more of these charities coming from Britain than from any other country. Apparently these charities provide around 40,000 jobs in the UK, and five out of the eleven largest international charities in the world began in the UK.

Why is this? Well, you might not be surprised at the answer by now – the British Empire. As we now know, Britain has a very long history of getting involved in other nations' business. Indeed, you can't get more 'involved' in another country than taking it over! And while colonization often gave Britain more power and money, at the time many British people also believed that it was good for the colonized people too.

Britain saw itself as better than other countries and more 'civilized', and felt it was its duty to teach 'lesser' countries. So colonizers would go around trying to spread British values. For example, they would spread Christianity throughout a country, changing its laws and customs so they were more in tune with British ones. Also, after Britain abolished the slave trade in its empire, in 1807, it was very keen to abolish slavery in other countries (as you may recall from Chapter 7).

Driven by this desire to 'do good', many British charities, or INGOs (which stands for international

CHAPTER 8

non-governmental organizations), such as Save the Children, were established during the days of the British Empire, and continue to work today. And of course many of them do very important work. I mean, who *doesn't* believe that we should save children? (OK, maybe not *all* children. We can leave out your annoying sibling.)

The difficulty came when charities did not just help or protect those in need, but tried to force British or Western values on a place and interfered with its own customs and culture. When they thought that 'the West knows best'.

One example of this is when Save the Children created schools in Africa to spread British values in the 1940s and 1950s after the Second World War. Some of these schools were basically prisons, with children suffering from beatings and being left in rooms all on their own as punishments.

There were also environmental charities that, among other things, worked to turn large areas of the countryside across the empire into national parks. Of course, that sounds great from over here - we like the idea of protecting wild animals and nature from damage - and these organizations did some amazing work. But often the British had caused the damage in the first place. And if you turn an area into a national park, the people who live there are sometimes forced to leave their homes. They are no longer able to use the land for farming or grazing their animals. Sometimes they were even fined or put in prison for continuing their old way of life. Complicated, isn't it?

CHAPTER 9

The Younghusband Expedition to Tibet, 1903–04

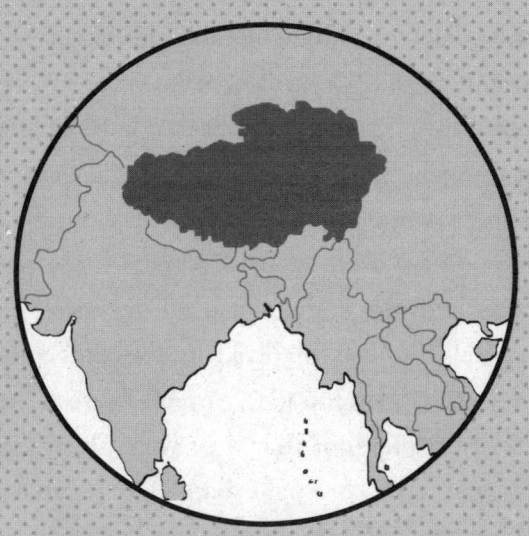

CHAPTER 9

Lieutenant Colonel Sir Francis Edward Younghusband. A lot of funny titles, and a funny long name, for a funny bloke, with a very long and funny life. By 'funny' I mean 'peculiar', of course. Even by the standards of the Victorian age, which produced many strange adventurers who had a thing for moustaches so fancy that they sometimes resembled small animals, Francis was a bit of a character.

His achievements during his seventy-nine years of life included getting the world record for the 300-yard dash (the modern version would be running 200 metres, I suppose, though 300 yards is actually 274.32 metres, which isn't such a snappy number!). He became one of the first Europeans to travel from Peking to Central Asia (he went across the Gobi Desert, through a part of the world now known as Mongolia and China, over the Himalayas and into India – a total distance of about 3,000 miles!). He was involved in the climber George Mallory's efforts to conquer Mount Everest. And he wrote thirty books (not that they were always good – one reviewer said: 'Younghusband has written many books, each one worse than the one before.').

But the thing I want to tell you about is the Younghusband Expedition, when Francis led a British mission to Tibet between 1903 and 1904. I want to tell

THE YOUNGHUSBAND EXPEDITION TO TIBET, 1903-04

you about it because its name does not really convey what it involved. The word 'expedition' makes it sound like a geography field trip, but I can guarantee it was much more ambitious, controversial and bloody than your average school trip to the Lake District.

I also want to tell you about it because it caused a sensation at the time. The British public were fascinated by Tibet, which is located in the Himalayas, a mountain range in Asia, and the highest region on earth. This made it extremely hard to get to, and its borders were often closed to foreigners, which meant very few Europeans had ever been there. It was seen as a very mysterious, even mystical place. A kind of combination of Mars, the Door of Night in *The Lord of the Rings*, and the drawer where everyone in the family puts unclaimed wires and phone chargers.

At forty, Francis wasn't actually that young, even for a grown-up, when he went to Tibet. He was indeed a husband, to a woman called Helen, although she sensibly stayed at home with their daughter when he charged off on his wild mission. Instead, he was accompanied to Tibet by around 4,000 men, mostly from the British Indian Army, which, as the name suggests, was the main military force in British-run India, and made up of both Europeans and Indians. Also present was a medical

officer and archaeologist called Dr Laurence Waddell, an expert on Tibet, who was something of a real-life Indiana Jones.* (Dr Waddell was another dashing Victorian eccentric. He had previously tried to reach Lhasa, the capital of Tibet, in 1892, in disguise as a Tibetan man, but his blue eyes had given him away.)

The official aim of the mission was to help smooth over tensions between Tibet and a neighbouring Indian state called Sikkim. But this wasn't the real motivation. India was the 'Jewel in the Crown' of Britain's colonies by this time, which means it was its most valuable territory. And Britain wanted to defend the territory at all costs, even more ferociously than when you have a plate of chips and you're very hungry and a sibling is determined to steal some.

As we learned in Chapter 6, the British were very worried about the Russians, who were also expanding their empire in the region. They wanted to make sure that Tibet would not fall under Russian influence. To be more accurate, they wanted to enter the forbidden land,

---

* What do you mean you've never heard of Indiana Jones? He was the greatest fictional American professor, archaeologist and adventurer of all time! If you haven't seen the Indiana Jones films yet, you're in for a treat. *Raiders of the Lost Ark* and *Indiana Jones and the Last Crusade* are must-sees.

CHAPTER 9

force Tibet to open its borders to trade, and establish British influence in the country.

But if the Younghusband Expedition was meant to calmly persuade the Tibetans to side with the British, it failed spectacularly. Tibet's leaders were suspicious of the British and refused to enter into discussion. In response, the British crushed them, with huge military force. There were sixteen battles, during which up to 3,000 Tibetans died; one eyewitness described the Tibetans as being 'knocked over like skittles'.

The Tibetans were Buddhist, a religion that usually rejects violence. They had an army but were not ready to fight such violent battles. Among other things, the Tibetans tried to protect themselves by wearing *gaus*, which are a type of amulet or lucky charm. And when the British Indian Army unleashed machine-gun fire upon them, the battle was very one-sided, and they defeated the Tibetans quickly and brutally.

You might have heard of the Dalai Lama, which is the title given to the spiritual leader of Tibet. Well, when the Dalai Lama of the time fled from the violence, the British took advantage of his absence by making Tibetan officials sign a document called the Treaty of Lhasa. Like the machine gun vs lucky charms battles, this treaty was wildly one-sided and unfair. It insisted that Tibet should have no relationship with any other foreign power (in other words, with Russia), that it should accept trade with British India, and that it should pay a large amount of money to Britain because the British were 'forced' to invade them. Imagine if someone beat you up, and then made you sign a document saying that from now on you'd only be friends with them and no one else, and that you'd give them all your pocket money until further notice because it was somehow *your* fault that they attacked you! That's basically what the treaty did.

But the British weren't just interested in taking cold, hard cash from Tibet. Perhaps more than almost any other imperial journey, the expedition is infamous for its looting. As you might have gathered from earlier chapters, 'loot' is the term for when people steal things from the places that they attack or occupy. It actually comes from the Hindi word for 'spoils of war' (the imperialists stole so much that they even stole the word, you could say).

As the British were fascinated by this mysterious, isolated land in the clouds, many of those who took part in the Younghusband Expedition could not resist taking 'souvenirs' home with them. Quite a few 'souvenirs' actually. Tibetan artefacts that made their way back to Britain included Buddha statues, painted scrolls, prayer

CHAPTER 9

wheels, amber, diamonds, jewel-encrusted artworks, gold crowns, earrings, necklaces and tiger skins. Not quite the same as when you bring back a fridge magnet from your holiday in Spain.

Officially this taking/stealing of 'souvenirs' – or 'looting', to give it its proper name – was forbidden. In fact, when two men were caught stealing gold images from a nunnery, Dr Waddell (the Indiana Jones man) ordered the images to be returned, and the men were given prison sentences. However, this is where things get confusing, because *Dr Waddell himself* also 'collected' lots of precious items.

You see, there was a sneaky law in place about the spoils of war, which basically said that if indigenous people resisted the British, then it was OK to take their stuff. So, as the Tibetans had originally defended the town of Gyantse Jong from the British invaders, this meant that the British could 'legally' take the precious things they found there. Which is a bit like saying a robber is allowed to steal everything in your house because you tried not to let them into your house in the first place.

Also, Dr Waddell had been given some money by the British Indian government to buy objects of interest: in total 10,000 rupees, which was and still is the currency used in the region. With that he ended up buying more than 2,000 precious items, such as porcelain, manuscripts, paintings and weaponry. He needed 400 mules (a cross between a donkey and a horse) to transport all this 'shopping'. If he had 10,000 rupees and bought 2,000 things, that means he paid on average just five rupees per item. You don't need to know exactly how much a rupee was worth back then to know that he was not paying the Tibetans a fair price for their treasures. Lots of people today consider what happened as theft.

Some of this precious loot from the Younghusband Expedition is still on display in British museums today, alongside many other objects that have been taken in murky ways. As we discovered on page 56, the fact that some (though not all) artefacts in British museums were taken in these immoral ways is something that people continue to argue and debate about. Many believe that these objects should be given back to the people or places they were taken from (this is called *restitution*). Yet others disagree. And, in any case, the British Museum is often not allowed to give its objects back – there is an actual law forbidding it in lots of cases. At least the museum is honest about the artefacts from this expedition, though, because labels state that 'many were forcibly taken by military officers'.

CHAPTER 9

There are many other examples of loot in British museums. Perhaps the most famous is Tipu's Tiger (which I wrote about in my last book, *Stolen History*), an almost life-sized mechanical model of a European soldier being mauled by a tiger, which was looted from the ruler of Mysore in southern India in 1799. You can still see it in the Victoria and Albert Museum.

This all sounds quite horrible, I know. British troops invading a country, killing those who tried to resist them and then stealing their stuff, and the Tibetan expedition was a dark moment of the British Empire. But I want to let you know that at the time even some British people who were huge fans of the British Empire frowned upon the looting. When the authorities became aware of what had happened in Tibet, some newspapers expressed their outrage, and Lord Kitchener, the head of the army, issued orders against further looting.

And what of Lieutenant Colonel Sir Francis Edward Younghusband, the leader of the expedition? I promised you he was a peculiar person, and perhaps he hasn't sounded very odd so far. But he had a wild life outside this wild 'expedition'. Not least, he became extremely spiritual, and a firm believer in the 'power of cosmic rays'. Don't ask me what this means. Not many people followed him at the time. He became confident that there was a planet called Altair, which was inhabited by aliens with see-through flesh. And, perhaps most surprisingly for a man who was an agent of the British Empire, he later became a strong supporter of Indian independence (Indians running their own country themselves).

CHAPTER 9

IMPERIAL HOTELS

Rome wasn't built in a day, as the saying goes - and neither was Britain's empire. The people who spread British influence across the world, and the people who visited them, needed somewhere to sleep. So if you travel today to a major city, in a country once colonized by the British, the chances are that you'll find a big fancy hotel that was built for just that purpose.

One of the most famous is called Raffles in Singapore. Sir Thomas Stamford Raffles founded the port of Singapore in 1819, and the hotel that bears his name began life as a modest ten-bedroom bungalow in 1887. It was very popular because it had a great location near the beach, and over

the years more and more buildings were added to it. Today it is one of the world's most luxurious hotels. And in the Singapore Grand Prix, Formula 1 drivers whizz past at it up to 200 miles an hour.

Among the many bars and restaurants at Raffles Hotel is its Writers Bar, where guests can order a Billion Dollar Cocktail. OK, it actually costs slightly less than a billion dollars – a mere $88, which is approximately £50. Still, £50, for one drink! You could get a lot of Fanta for that. More than eighty-three cans, in fact.

Hold on, are you now thinking of becoming a writer, because they're all clearly so loaded? I feel it is my duty to tell you that, despite the name of the bar, most writers don't make enough money to spend that much on drinks all night long! Anyway, back to our subject.

Another iconic imperial hotel is the Great Eastern Hotel in Kolkata. It was established in the 1840s when the city was the headquarters

CHAPTER 9

of the East India Company. In its heyday the hotel was the centre of colonial life in the city, and everything could be found there. Unusually for a hotel at the time you could go shopping inside. It contained a kind of department store called the Hall for All Nations where you could buy almost anything you wanted.

Other imperial hotels that still stand today include Shepheard's in Cairo, Egypt (the original one burned down in 1952, and a new one, called the Shepheard Hotel, was built nearby soon afterwards); the Grand Oriental in Colombo, Sri Lanka; and, in India, the Taj Mahal Palace in Mumbai and the Imperial in Delhi. These places all had the reputation of offering everything under the sun. But, in some cases, that was only the case if you were white. Yes, unfortunately, some of them had racist policies. Even if non-white people were allowed into the hotel, they were often treated badly, ignored or served cold food, and so they didn't want to return.

THE YOUNGHUSBAND EXPEDITION TO TIBET, 1903-04

Nowadays these places will serve anyone, as long as they can pay for it. And if you're the kind of person who can afford £50 drinks, you don't have to go to Singapore or Sri Lanka to experience a lavish colonial hotel. In a neat twist, a branch of Raffles Hotel has recently opened in London in the building that used to house the War Office, where former prime minister Winston Churchill and other figures of Empire used to walk the corridors.

Personally the drinks are a little too expensive for me – I'd prefer eighty-three cans of Fanta!

CHAPTER 10
A Luxurious Trip to India, 1911–12

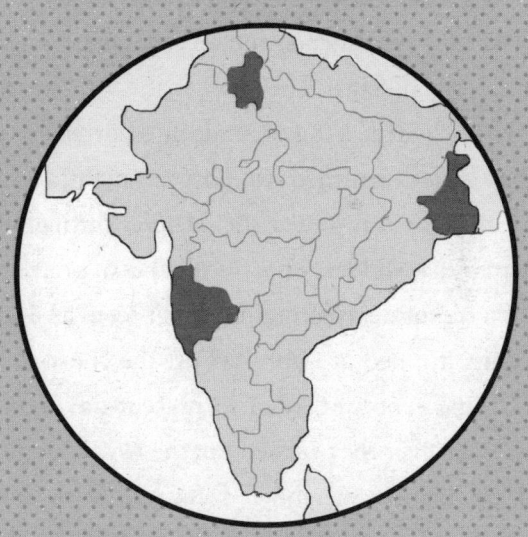

CHAPTER 10

What's the most luxurious journey you've been on? Even if you have travelled on a private jet to the Caribbean, and then been picked up on arrival in a Rolls-Royce limousine, and then stayed in an enormous villa packed with beautiful puppies and playful kittens, it still won't have been as extravagant as King George V and Queen Mary's trip to India between 1911 and 1912.

They travelled on the RMS *Medina*, which was a newly built ocean liner that had been especially improved for the royal visit. The large public rooms inside had been refitted as royal apartments, and an extra mast was added for special royal flags. The ship, with 733 passengers and crew on board, left Portsmouth escorted by fifteen warships, which returned to port at nightfall, except for four cruisers that joined the *Medina* throughout the journey to India. Suddenly the free packet of pretzels I was given on a recent delayed flight doesn't seem as exciting.

The ship stopped at Gibraltar off the coast of Spain, Port Said in Egypt and Aden in present-day Yemen on the way. Wherever they turned up, the royal couple were greeted by British warships decorated with bunting, and visits from local rulers and British officials. The last three days at sea were spent playing sports on board: three-legged races, obstacle courses and pillow fights on a greasy pole (they'd bash each other with a pillow until someone fell off). The voyage took them three weeks. Queen Mary got seasick, and so had a swinging cot installed to help her feel better. (I might try to get one of those next time I go on a ferry!)

Finally the *Medina* steamed into Bombay, greeted by a 101-gun salute (a military tradition that involves firing weapons to celebrate a big event – basically a giant version of party poppers). Special pavilions had been built at the harbour for the royal couple's arrival. At the port there was a 'Children's Festival' with 25,000 flag-waving children. The king and queen drove past in a carriage accompanied by guards and Scottish bagpipers, while the national anthem was sung in four languages.

They then took a train to Delhi – it took thirty-six hours to travel the 982 miles. And they arrived on 7 December at a station that had been built specially for the occasion. You may have heard the rumour that when Queen Elizabeth II visited certain places, they put in a new toilet seat just for her? Well, this was like that – and then some! Everywhere the royal couple went, huge crowds turned out to see them.

Throughout, the king travelled with the Imperial Crown of India, which had been created especially for the trip. He already had another suitable crown,

CHAPTER 10

the Imperial State Crown, but the law states that the Crown Jewels are not allowed to leave the country. (It's a strange law, some might say, given that the Crown Jewels include so many jewels bought, gifted or taken from other countries.) So a near copy of it was made especially for the India visit, except it was a lighter version because of the country's hot weather.

Someone from the royal jewellers that made the crown also joined the trip in case the crown needed any last-minute changes. It was covered with 6,100 diamonds as well as emeralds, rubies and sapphires, and cost £60,000 to make, which is nearly £8 million in today's money! At the time of writing, the average house price in England is about £300,000, so you could buy roughly twenty-six and a half houses for the price of this crown that was only worn once. Or eighty brand-new Porsche 911s. Or, if you're not into houses or cars, 9,411,764 Mars bars. Bonkers!

This cash did not come from the king but from the Indian government. The crown has long been a very important symbol of royalty, and the purpose of the visit was to put on a great show to celebrate British rule of India, so the king needed a very impressive jewel-encrusted crown. More precisely, the king and queen were there to attend a spectacular event called the Delhi

A LUXURIOUS TRIP TO INDIA, 1911–12

Durbar. It took place around the time the British Empire was at its biggest and boldest, and at it the king and queen were named the emperor and empress of India.

What's a Durbar? Well, before I can answer this, we need to go back to the 1600s when the British first arrived in India with the East India Company. The company was set up to help Britain make money from selling spices like cloves, ginger, nutmeg, cinnamon and saffron around the world – this was called the global spice trade and Britain wanted a piece of the action. But over time the company became an extension of the British government, complete with an army that, at one point, was twice the size of the actual British army. Their mission was to take control of other territories.

By the middle of the nineteenth century, much of the country was ruled by the East India Company. The company was cruel, ruthless and not very popular, and in 1857, there was a violent uprising among Indians against it. The rebellion was brutally quashed, but it was decided that the company should officially hand over control of its territories to the British government. The rebellion marked the start of resistance against British rule, as Britain slowly began to realize that the best people to run India were the Indians themselves.

So, aware of the potential for unrest, the British

CHAPTER 10

wanted to keep the population quiet and loyal. They tried to push the message that India, and the other countries in the empire, were all part of one big happy family, with the British royal family at its head. And George's royal tour, with the Durbar as its highlight, was an opportunity to put out that message of belonging.

Durbars were lavish gatherings put on by the Mughal emperors who largely ruled India before the British took over. At these ceremonies the Muslim ruler would display his wealth and power, and local leaders would show their loyalty to him. Now that the British were the ultimate rulers of the country, they had decided to adopt the tradition, in the hope it would show to Britain, India and the rest of the world that Indian people loved them and wanted them there.

George and Mary were not the first British monarchs to claim the title of emperor or empress of India, but they were the first to attend the Durbar. Queen Victoria was named empress in 1877, and King Edward VII was named emperor in 1903, but they both sent viceroys (the top-ranking British official in India) to the ceremony in their place. Wouldn't it be nice if we could all send out people to represent us in this way? You'd never have to go to another school assembly or do another cross-country run . . .

King George was looking very regal on 12 December during his coronation ceremony at the Durbar. He wore the same purple and ermine robes that he had worn to his coronation in London in the summer, and, of course, his new Imperial Crown of India. Around 100,000 spectators were waiting for them. The couple were seated on thrones on a platform under a golden canopy and George described the scene before him as 'the most beautiful and wondrous sight I ever saw'. But privately he complained about the heat and the weight of his crown, even though it had been made lighter for him. He moaned in his diary: 'Rather tired after wearing the crown for 3½ hours; it hurt my head, as it is pretty heavy . . .'

Among all this pomp, the coronation ceremony itself only lasted an hour. The king gave a speech in which he made two announcements. One was that East and West Bengal would be brought back together. The background to this was that in 1905, the British government had divided up the Indian region of Bengal, which, with 80 million inhabitants, was their largest territory. This decision had been controversial and had angered those who wanted the British to stop interfering with India. The second announcement was that the capital of India would be moved from Calcutta to Delhi. This was significant because Calcutta had been the headquarters

CHAPTER 10

of the East India Company, which was strongly disliked, and so the move to Delhi signalled a break from the past. These two announcements were made to please those who were against British rule, by showing that the British were listening to Indian concerns.

The announcements also show that, even at a time when the king was being celebrated and the British Empire was peaking in size, cracks were beginning to show. Another sign that all was not totally well involved a guest at the Durbar, a local Indian ruler, the gaekwar of Baroda. Before the Durbar many of the invited Indian leaders had been awarded titles, honours and medals. This was to make them feel proud and warm towards the king. They were given titles such as Knight Grand Commander, Knight Commander and Knight Grand Cross as acknowledgement of their rank and loyalty to the British. But the gaekwar of Baroda had not been awarded the knighthood he expected – probably because he was openly in favour of Indian independence.

However, despite his views, he had always been loyal to the emperor and felt very annoyed and insulted. So, at the Durbar, when it was his turn to pay his respects to the royal couple, the gaekwar of Baroda decided to make a bold statement. First, unlike the other Indian leaders, he wasn't wearing all his finery. He had arrived wearing his finest jewels, but removed them before he approached the throne. Then, after a quick bow, he turned his back and walked away. Now, turning your back on a monarch or emperor was seen as disrespectful. That's why in films you often see people shuffling backwards out of rooms after meeting a monarch. It was widely seen as a slight, or a diss, and an act of opposition to British rule. Awks!

The coronation itself may have been short but there were many more lavish ceremonies for the king and queen to sit through. The next day, they made a balcony appearance at the Red Fort in Delhi, in front of a crowd estimated at *half a million*. This is a bigger crowd than even Taylor Swift has played for. Next came a military inspection of 40,000 troops (where soldiers have their uniforms and skills assessed), and a cavalry charge (a re-enactment of a military tactic where mounted soldiers rush towards the enemy in close combat). Then came another ceremony in front of a huge crowd . . . Well, you get the idea.

After that the royal couple were allowed a holiday in nearby Nepal. The purpose of this 'holiday' was hunting. The prime minister of Nepal made available some 600 elephants and 14,000 beaters (people who go around hitting bushes and things to make animals move).

A LUXURIOUS TRIP TO INDIA, 1911-12

Bait was put out for tigers, a thirteen-mile road was built along the valley of the Rui River, and a special bungalow with electric light was constructed for King George to sleep in. On his most 'successful' day of hunting, King George killed four tigers and one bear. Of course, this was not very successful for the animals involved, especially as tigers are now a critically endangered species.

The couple were there over Christmas, and guess what the king was given as a present by his hosts? A baby rhino! He didn't shoot this animal but shipped it back to London Zoo. After their holiday, the king and queen visited Calcutta, and then took the train to Bombay and got back on board the RMS *Medina* for the journey home.

By this time film had been invented, which meant the public were able to see moving pictures of the trip, rather than just read about it in newspaper reports. The colour feature film of the trip, titled *With Our King and Queen Through India*, was shown in cinemas shortly after they returned to the UK. In those days there weren't very many film options available. It wasn't like today, when *With Our King and Queen Through India* would have to compete with *Deadpool & Wolverine Redux* and the *Minions Go Crazy in Vegas* and *Spider-Man 18*.

CHAPTER 10

But cinema had only just been invented, and so the two-and-a-half-hour-long film *With Our King and Queen Through India* was considered very exciting.

So, apart from the little hiccup with the snub by the gaekwar of Baroda, the royal trip was seen as a success in Britain. It was thought it would encourage Indians to want to stick with British rule. But as it turned out, George and Mary would not only be the first monarchs to visit Britain's Indian empire but also the last. It would only continue for another thirty-six years, until 1947.

Why? Well, history buffs will know that, very soon after the royal trip, came an event that turned the whole world upside down: the First World War. More than a million Indian troops fought for Britain in the war, and afterwards nothing would be the same for the British Indian Empire. Voices of opposition, in favour of Indian independence, would grow louder and louder. One of the most famous voices of opposition led our next journey – one which was significantly less luxurious than anything the king, queen, or you and I have probably ever experienced.

TIME

Would you rather be the size of an elephant for the rest of your life or the size of a mouse? Who would win in a fight between Harry Potter and Captain America? The world is full of tricky questions but 'What time is it?' is not one of them. You just look at a working clock and that's the time! Right now, as I'm writing this, it's 10.13 a.m. It's the same for anyone else in the UK.

But of course different countries are in different time zones. There are twenty-four international time zones in total, one for each hour of the day. So, for example, Madrid in Spain is one hour ahead of London, and New York on the east coast of the USA is five hours behind London.

Once upon a time (ha!), it wasn't so straightforward. At all! Many people told the time by the position of the sun, using an instrument called a sundial that gave the time depending on

CHAPTER 10

where the sun cast its shadow. This meant that time varied not just from country to country but from town to town, even within the UK. The further west you lived, the later your day started, because the time of day depends on where you are in relation to the sun. So Bristol, say, was ten minutes behind London. This sort of worked, when people kept to their local areas. But then in the nineteenth century people started moving around a lot more, and the world needed to tell the time more precisely.

One of the reasons for this was because rail travel had been invented, and people needed to know exactly when the trains would leave and arrive. Imagine people with different concepts of time trying to catch trains? Chaos! There were also more ships travelling around the world that needed a precise time to be able to calculate where they were on the planet exactly. They would use a device called a chronometer, which is an extremely accurate clock used for navigation. At Greenwich in London the Royal Observatory sent out a regular time signal (and still does today). At 1 p.m. every day, a large red ball dropped down a mast placed on top of the observatory, so that ships moored in the docks below could set their chronometers precisely.

And for the British Empire and other empires, this was especially important; it meant they could spread information and keep control better. In the same way that it helps a head teacher run a school if every lesson begins and ends at the same time.

The time had come (ha!) for a standardized global system of time. In 1884, an international conference of twenty-eight countries was held in the USA. Here it was decided that the world's time would be set and measured from Greenwich's Prime Meridian. This is an imaginary line that runs from the North Pole to the South Pole, passing through Greenwich. If you are to the east of the Prime Meridian, the time is ahead of London; if you are to the west, the time is behind London.

CHAPTER 10

This meant that all global time would be set in relation to the time in Greenwich – they called this Greenwich Mean Time (or GMT). And GMT became Britain's official time. It was chosen largely because Britain was so important, due to its massive empire and the huge influence Britain had across the world.

In 1852, a 'master clock' was installed in Greenwich to set the time, and it was linked to four 'slave clocks', including one at London Bridge railway station. The use of words like 'master' and 'slave', which were so key to the British Empire, was another sign of how important empire was to the development of global standardized time.

From 1866 the Greenwich clock sent time signals via underwater cables to Harvard University in the USA (see page 125). And by the early twentieth century, most countries had adopted time zones that used GMT. So the time in Madrid was GMT+1, and New York GMT-5. In the modern world, GMT has now been replaced by UTC, which stands for Coordinated Universal Time – even though the letters are in the wrong order (it should be CUT, surely?). But GMT and UTC are the same time. Confused? Me too. Time after time!

CHAPTER II
Gandhi and the Salt March, 1930

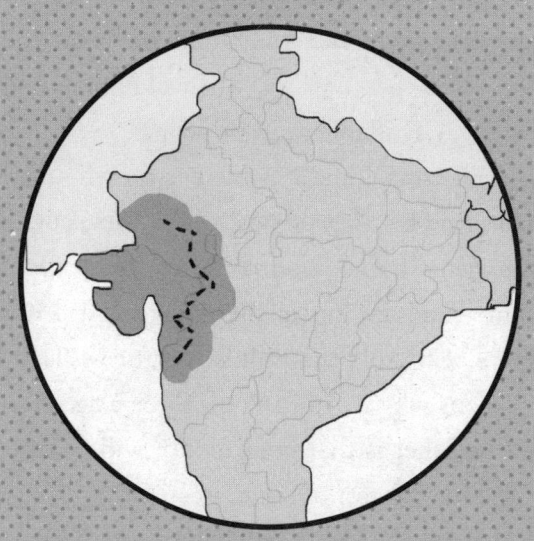

CHAPTER 11

Here's a game. Fill in the missing word in the following phrase: 'Next to air and water, _____ is perhaps the greatest necessity of life.' Love? Money? Haribo? Double geography? A book about the world's most interesting imperial journeys?

Whatever your answer, I bet it says something about you! It also quite possibly says something about the time you live in. For instance, if you said 'TV' this tells me that that you are definitely a modern person. 'A spinning wheel' might suggest that you were a cloth maker in the seventeenth century, and 'a chamber pot' that you were from the eighteenth century, when plumbing and flush toilets weren't available to most people.

Well, Mahatma Gandhi is the person who made that statement. And his answer was . . . salt! Yes, salt. I know. The statement sounds kind of weird. Not only does it seem quite random, but in the twenty-first century we are always being told that salt is bad for us. That is one of the reasons why we mustn't eat three bags of crisps in one go (the other is that your mouth will be drier than the Sahara for the rest of the day).

Well, it's true that too much salt is bad for us. But we do need to eat it sometimes. Salt helps balance the amount of water in the body, and this is particularly important in hot countries, such as India, where Gandhi was from, where you might sweat a lot. But Gandhi was not just trying to raise awareness about our need for salt. His answer definitely tells us something about the time he lived in.

In 1930, when Gandhi made this statement, the British had ruled India for a long time. In order to get money from the Indian citizens, they imposed large taxes on many products, including salt. This meant every time someone bought salt, they had to pay an extra amount of money, on top of the price, to the government. The Salt Act of 1882 banned everyone from producing or selling salt themselves, so Indians had no choice but to buy it from the government at a high price.

This was something the British often did in their colonies; they would control the production and sale of a product, and then they would sell it back to its colonized people at whatever price they chose. But the decision to do this on salt was particularly controversial. Salt was not a luxury, like diamonds, or wine or a Nintendo Switch; it was an essential food for Indian people, and they needed it to survive, and the prices the British charged for it were too high for many to afford.

There had been protests against the salt tax, but none had much impact until Gandhi got involved. Getting attention was something he was very good at. And so,

CHAPTER 11

in 1930, he organized a march in protest against the salt tax. As he saw it, salt was an important, ordinary part of everyday life, and the British control over it showed how much the Indian population was being exploited by them. The march marked the start of Gandhi's famous campaign against British rule, called *satyagraha*, or 'insistence upon truth'. And this eventually led to India's independence in 1947.

Before I tell you about this extraordinary march, let's go back to Mahatma Gandhi himself. You'll probably have heard of him or seen pictures of him before – he had a very distinctive look, with his bald head, round glasses and shawl. He dressed in the simple traditional Indian clothes that many Indian workers, including those who became indentured labourers in places like British Guiana, wore. There are movies about his incredible life and a statue of him in Parliament Square in London. But you might not be entirely sure about who he was.

First off, Mahatma wasn't his actual name. 'Mahatma' was a title given to him, which means 'venerable', another word for 'respected'. His real name was Mohandas Karamchand Gandhi, and he was born into a Hindu family in the Indian state of Gujarat in 1869. Aged eighteen, he moved to London to train as a lawyer. He had been raised a vegetarian, and so promised his mum that he wouldn't eat meat in London, which he found tricky – there were no Quorn nuggets in Victorian London! But then he discovered the London Vegetarian Society, and even wrote for their magazine *The Vegetarian*.

Once Gandhi had qualified as a lawyer, he worked in South Africa for twenty-one years, becoming involved in the civil rights movement there – the battle against racism and the campaign for equal rights for Black people. On returning to India, he joined the political party the Indian National Congress, which was in favour of Indian independence from Britain. Soon he became the party's leader.

From 1919 to 1922 he led something called the 'non-cooperation movement' (perhaps you could say you're a member of this movement, the next time you're asked to turn off the TV and do your homework). The movement was set up as a non-violent one, focusing on not buying British services and goods. Gandhi encouraged Indians to buy home-produced goods and services rather than British ones to protest against the way that the British were making money from the country.

The protest was non-violent, but this ended in 1922 when the police began shooting at protestors. They responded by setting fire to a police station and killing

CHAPTER 11

everyone inside. Nineteen of the violent protestors were sentenced to death by the colonial authorities. (Gandhi did not support the attack.)

Gandhi himself then spent some time in prison for his activities aimed at questioning and undermining British rule. He was arrested on charges of sedition, which meant the British thought he was encouraging rebellion. And, following this, he took some time away from politics.

In 1930, protestors wrote a list of demands to the British viceroy, which included abolishing the salt tax. When this was ignored, Gandhi got the idea for his march. Appropriately enough the march began in the month of March – 12 March, to be precise. Gandhi and around eighty others set off from his ashram, or spiritual retreat, in a place called Sabermati. They were heading for a village called Dandi, which was 240 miles away. He had chosen Dandi as his destination not because it rhymes with Gandhi but because it was on the Arabian Sea, where salt was found. The plan was to collect salt from the beach there, and so publicly disobey the British ban on Indians collecting the stuff.

In case you were wondering, yes, they could have caught the train to Dandi, rather than walking all that way! But Gandhi knew that marching would attract lots of attention. Also, marching was symbolic; in both Indian and Western mythology, a march is associated with making a sacrifice for an important cause.

Gandhi was sixty-one at the time, the oldest person on the march, and he walked in the shawl and sandals he was famous for (along with a stick). He set a brisk pace, and on the first day he and his men covered about 13 miles. Stopping for the night in a village, Gandhi gave a speech to the locals about what they were doing. His inspiring words helped them collect more supporters, and this continued each day, until there were thousands of people walking with him.

The march and the route had been announced in advance, so newspapers and film crews from around the world reported its progress. When they entered a new village, they were welcomed by crowds with drums and cymbals. In the evenings, Gandhi made speeches to great gatherings of supporters. The marchers wore simple white clothes like Gandhi and they slept outside, but were provided with food and water by the villagers. And on 5 April, twenty-four days after setting off, the march finally reached Dandi.

The next morning Gandhi and others broke the law by picking up handfuls of salt from the beach. Holding up a lump of salt, he gave another good quote: 'With

CHAPTER 11

this, I am shaking the foundations of the British Empire!' Gandhi was not arrested that day, as the authorities feared a backlash from his supporters if he was, but over the coming days other campaigners were, including a man called Jawaharlal Nehru. He was a fellow member of the Indian National Congress who went on to become prime minister when India was granted independence in 1947.

(A side note: like his friend Gandhi, Nehru had what you might call a 'signature look': in his case, a jacket with a short, sticking-up collar. The style caught on, and when the English rock band The Beatles started wearing them, so-called 'Nehru suits' became hugely popular in the west as well as India, and remain so today.)

Back to Gandhi. He continued his *satyagraha*, urging people to join him in breaking the salt laws in a non-violent protest against British rule. But when he planned another march on a saltworks (a place where salt was produced for sale) he too was arrested, and by the end of 1930, at least 60,000 people involved in the protests had been imprisoned. Gandhi negotiated with the British about ending the campaign from jail. According to a journalist, during one meeting he added a pinch of salt to a cup of tea, saying that he did so 'to remind us of the famous Boston Tea Party'.

CHAPTER 11

This was a snarky reference to the protest over tea taxes that kicked off America's revolt against British rule. In 1773, American demonstrators threw chests of tea into Boston Harbour in defiance of British taxes on tea and their rule in America. By saying this, Gandhi made it clear that the real aim of the marches was not just to reform the salt laws but to achieve independence for India.

Gandhi was released from jail in January 1931 after six months in prison. He entered into negotiations with Lord Irwin, the viceroy of India, and they signed an agreement on 5 March. As part of this, Gandhi would stop his campaign if the British released those they had imprisoned, allowed Indians to collect their own salt and let the Indian National Congress participate in talks about reforming British rule. Some of his supporters were disappointed by this result, and felt it hadn't gone far enough. However, the impact of the march went way beyond that agreement, and beyond India itself.

Gandhi and his supporters became symbols of resistance to oppression across the world. Gandhi became *TIME* magazine's 'Man of the Year' – an honour given to the man who had had the greatest impact on the world. Before long the idea that you could make big changes through peaceful protest had spread around the world. Later, Martin Luther King, the famous American civil rights activist, fighting against racism, said he had been inspired by Gandhi.

The British were not so impressed – or, rather, they recognized that Gandhi was a real threat to British rule and so tried to destroy his reputation. Winston Churchill described Gandhi as a fanatic, who strode around 'half naked'. They were right to feel threatened. As with the Boston Tea Party in North America, Gandhi's march marked the beginning of the end of British rule in India. His negotiations with the British led to the Indian National Congress having 'a seat at the table', and discussions about reforming British rule made Britain realize that, finally, the game was over in India.

Gandhi did more than kickstart India's independence from Britain. He also worked to heal religious division in the country. He was able to unite Hindus and Muslims through their shared wish for India to rule itself, rather than be ruled by Britain. He also campaigned to improve the lives of the 'untouchables'. These people, now known as Dalits or Scheduled Caste, are members of the lowest caste in Hinduism's rigid system that organizes people into different categories.

This system says that Hindus are born into a social hierarchy (a sort of ladder where people are

CHAPTER 11

ranked based on things like their wealth and family background) that it is impossible to escape from. So, for instance, if you were born into the Dalit caste, you might have to be a street sweeper for your entire life, no matter how clever you were or how hard you worked. Gandhi refused to eat as a way to protest how unfair this system was. In 1933, he fasted for twenty-one days to protest against 'untouchability'. He also toured all India making speeches about the issue. But the outbreak of the Second World War in 1939 made him focus again on colonialism. The British had involved India in the war without consulting Indian leaders. In return for Indian help with the war, Gandhi demanded that the British leave India. However, it was only after the war, in 1945, that Britain, which was struggling financially and had a new prime minister, finally accepted that their time in India must come to an end.

At last! The moment Gandhi had been dreaming of. Well, not quite. Because the British decided that their final act in India would be to divide the country up into Muslim and Hindu states – an act called Partition that we learned about in Chapter 8. Gandhi had long campaigned for India's Muslims and Hindus to unite and he was strongly against this division. But, as we know, the plan went ahead anyway, and on 15 August

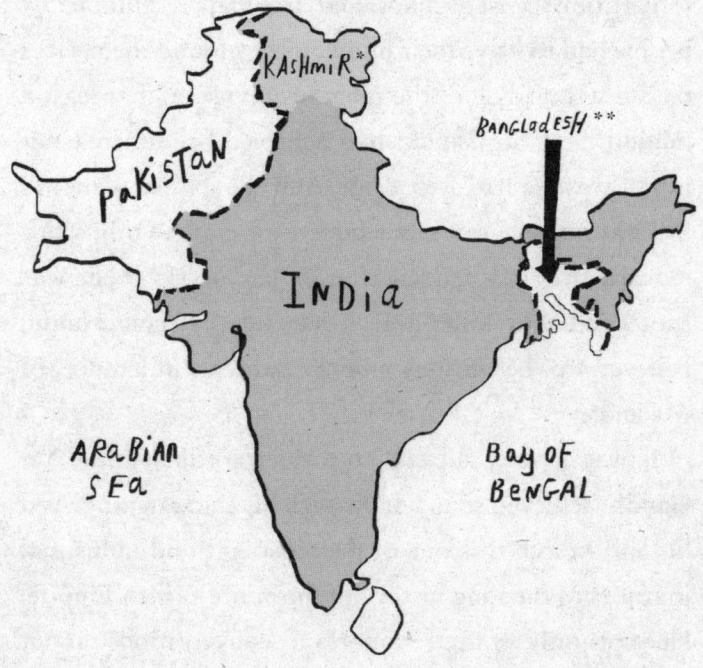

1947, India was separated into two countries, Hindu-majority India and Muslim-majority Pakistan, and both were granted their independence.

* The borders of Kashmir are disputed to this day by India and Pakistan.

** After Partition, this part of the world was known as East Bengal. It was renamed East Pakistan in 1956 and remained so until 1971. It became Bangladesh in 1971 after gaining independence from Pakistan.

CHAPTER 11

Partition caused chaos and trauma, as millions of people had to leave their homes if they found themselves on the wrong side of the religious divide, and at least a million died. So Gandhi had achieved his aim but not in the way he had hoped for. And the end of Gandhi's life was not what millions hoped for either. Only a few months after independence on 30 January 1948, he was shot dead. His killer was a hardline extreme Hindu, believed to be furious about Gandhi's tolerance of Muslims.

It was a very sad end to an extraordinary life. Yet Gandhi achieved so much through his campaigning. And his Salt March was one of the most epic and influential journeys in the long history of the entire British Empire. He not only started important conversations about Indian independence, but he also made sure that his fellow Indians could access an important mineral that is perhaps the greatest necessity of life, next to air and water and ... TV.

CONCLUSION

CONCLUSION

If you do anything for long enough, it can change your whole personality. Actors are often very dramatic people. Most dentists wouldn't dream of letting their children skip brushing their teeth. And some teachers can't help telling people what to do!

As for being a historian, my reply to pretty much *anything* nowadays is usually: 'Well, it's complicated.' I must have pointed out how complicated imperial history can be a dozen times in this book. And I say this a lot in conversation too.

What TV show shall we watch next? It's complicated.
What do you fancy for dinner tonight? It's complicated.
What's your favourite colour? It's complicated.

I hate hearing myself say this sometimes, but I can't help it because history, and the way it shapes our world today, *is* really complicated. Sometimes it is even contradictory – meaning lots of opposite things can be true at the same time, leaving you with all sorts of different feelings about it. Though this is an idea that I suspect children find easier to understand than adults. After all, you will know from your parents, guardians, siblings or friends that you can love people deeply and yet find them deeply, deeply irritating at the same time. The British Empire was contradictory like this.

CONCLUSION

It involved brutal slavery. At the same time, it also witnessed abolition, a campaign that saw the banning of slavery across the British Empire and beyond. The British Empire created all sorts of problems that are still felt today, in places like Palestine and Nigeria and Myanmar. But it also resulted in peace and democracy (a political system where people can have a say in how their country is run) in other parts of the world, such as Australia, New Zealand and Canada. Although it caused a huge amount of trauma, pain and death among the indigenous people living in these places.

Imperialists both put up and pulled down buildings. The British Empire both spread diseases among millions and helped millions survive them. It brought newspapers that shared important news, but then it blocked them from telling the truth. The British Empire spread racist attitudes and beliefs, but it also resulted in people of different ethnicities learning to live and work together. It displaced millions, yet gave millions of others work and shelter. In short, almost anything you say about it, you could say the opposite too.

While there are lots of simple facts about the history – and I hope you've learned some of them here – as I keep saying, it was also deeply complicated. In fact, people

CONCLUSION

will probably be arguing about the consequences of the British Empire for the rest of history!

From Ireland to North America, from Tibet to Iraq, the British Empire was created through monumental journeys that, in turn, changed the world forever. And the journeys themselves were as complicated as the empire. They were embarked on by people who did both good and bad things. They resulted in violence and death, but also freedom and independence.

So if there's one thing that I hope you have gained from reading this book, it is the courage to argue against simple statements. If someone says something very basic about the British Empire – such as 'it was all good' or 'it was all evil', I hope you'll be able to challenge them. I hope you'll say: 'Opposite things can be true at the same time.'

Or if you want to be a historian like me, you could use my favourite line of all:

'Actually it was complicated.'

QUESTIONS AND CONVERSATIONS ABOUT THE BRITISH EMPIRE

QUESTIONS AND CONVERSATIONS ABOUT THE BRITISH EMPIRE

As we have discovered, the subject of the British Empire is incredibly complicated. It's important not only to challenge what other people say about it, but also to challenge what you believe yourself. Changing your mind is a sign that you are always thinking and learning. To help, here are some questions and debates you could have at school or with friends, which could lead to important and positive discussions:

- Should Britain have compensated (paid) the enslaved people rather than slave owners when slavery was abolished?
- Should Britain now compensate the people whose ancestors were enslaved? This money is often referred to as *reparations*. Or has too much time passed?
- Should Britain apologize for what it did over the long history of the British Empire? What would be the effects of Britain apologizing?
- Should Britain return the loot in its museums, and the loot in the Crown Jewels, to the original owners? What would be the advantages and disadvantages of doing so?

- Should the national curriculum cover more of the history of the British Empire?
- When it comes to Olaudah Equiano, does it matter whether the story he tells in his memoir did not all happen to him?
- Should places renamed by British colonizers have their old indigenous names restored? What are the reasons for keeping an imperial place name as it is, and the reasons for changing it?
- Was Captain James Cook right to conclude that Australia was land belonging to no one? Did he seek the consent of the people already living there, as he was told to do?
- Should Britain still have honours like MBEs and CBEs that refer to the empire? If you think the titles should be changed, what should they be?
- What should the royal family do about all the ivory they own from the age of empire? And what about the furs and animal skins in their collections, which came from hunting animals across the British Empire?
- How would your daily life be different if the British Empire had not happened?

INDEX

A
abolitionist movement 52, 53–54, 90, 101, 116, 143
Aboriginal peoples 71, 72, 74, 75
Acknowledgement of Country 75
Africa 52–53, 80, 81–92, 144
see also Benin
Albert, Prince 96
Ali, Karamat 100–101
Altair 157
America *see* USA
Anglo-Normans 13
Anti-Slavery International 142
archaeology 135, 139
Argall, Samuel 35, 38
arguments 46–47
Armstrong, Neil 80
asking questions 202–203
astronomical unit 63
Australia 62, 64, 71–72, 74, 123, 203
Australian National Maritime Museum 69, 75
Austria 51

B
Banks, Joseph 62, 65–66, 68, 73–74, 75
Barbados 120
Batavia 73
Beatles 188
Bell, Gertrude 133–141
Bengal 99, 169
Benin 50, 52–53, 55–56
Benin Bronzes 55–56
Biafran War 112
Bingham, John 18
Bingham, Richard 18
Birmingham 41
borders 90–91, 112, 132
Boston, Massachusetts, USA 22
Boston Tea Party 188, 190
botany 65
Botany Bay 62, 72, 74
Bounty, HMS 78
Brazil 68
breadfruit 6, 62, 70, 74, 76–78

British Empire
  beginnings 4
  existence today 5
  imperial values 59, 84, 99, 143
  legacy 131–132, 139, 198–200
  size 2–3
  symbols 94
  timespan 4
British Indian Army 149
British Museum 55–56, 155
Buckingham Palace 93–94
Buddhism 152
Bukhara 102–108
Burton, Richard 85

C
cables, undersea 124, 125–126
Cairo 137, 160
Calcutta 169–170, 173
Camilla, Queen 96
Canada 112
Captain Kidd 11
Caribbean 77–78, 115
caste system 191–192
Catholicism 14–15
Central Asia 98, 101
Chambers, Anne 18
charities 6, 142–145
Charles III 96
child labour 68, 81
cholera 118
chronometers 176
Chuma, James 83, 86, 89
Churchill, Winston 191
civil rights movements 185, 191
clocks 178–179
cocktails 159
Colombo, Sri Lanka 160
colonialism
  Acknowledgement of Country 75
  brutality 33–34, 38–39, 71
  prisoner deportations 74
colonization, definition 3, 130
compensation payments to slave owners 117

Conolly, Arthur
  background 99–100
  Bukhara 103, 104–106
  death 99, 106
  early travels 100–101
  Great Game 98, 108
  intelligence office work 102
consensus 47
context, historical 13, 20
Cook, James 62, 64, 71, 72, 73, 75, 203
cosmic rays 156–157
cricket 58
croquet 57, 59
crossing the line 69–70
Crown Jewels 95, 165–167, 169, 202

D
Dalai Lama 152
Dalit caste 191–192
De Beers 91
debates 46–47, 202–203
dehumanization 53
Delhi 160, 165, 166–167, 169–171
Delhi Durbar 166–167, 168, 169–171
diamonds 82, 91, 95
diaspora 123
diplomacy 102–103
disease 23–24, 39–40, 49, 73, 74, 118, 199
Disney 30, 32, 38
Dorlton, George 68
Dublin 10, 13, 18
Durbars 166–167, 168, 169–171
dysentery 73

E
Earth, distance from the sun 63–64
East India Company 160, 167, 170
education
  on British Empire 5–6, 202–203
  women 133–134
Edward VI 14
Edward VII 168

Egypt 137, 160
Elizabeth I 4, 14, 18, 19, 28
emancipation 116
empire, definition of word 3–4
Endeavour, HMS 62, 66–73, 74–75, 76
English Channel 125
English language 22
enslavement 47–55
environmental charities 144–145
equality 140–141, 185
equator 69–70
Equiano, Olaudah 50–55, 203
exceptionalism 141, 143
exploration
   Australia and New Zealand 70–72
   David Livingstone early adventures 81–83
   exploitation 91–92
   Nile source 80, 85–89, 92
   Zambezi River 84–85

F
Facebook 19
Faisal, King 138
famines 23
films
   baddies played by British actors 21–22, 25
   With Our King and Queen Through India 173–174
First Fleet 74
First World War 137–138, 174
Flower, Peter 68
food and Empire 6, 77–78
football 57–58
France 15, 51
Frankopan, Peter 103

G
gaekwar of Baroda 170–171
galleys (ships) 11
Gandhi, Mahatma 182–185, 186–188, 190–194
George III 43, 65
George V 164, 165–167, 168, 169–173
Gladstone, John 117–118
Gladstone, William 117, 121
goats 68
Gobi Desert 148
Grand Oriental, Colombo 160
Great Eastern Hotel, Kolkata 159–160
Great Game 98, 99

Greenwich Mean Time (GMT) 177–179
Greenwich, Royal Observatory 176–177
grog shops 120
gutta-percha 124–125, 127–128
Guyana 115, 118–122

H
haemorrhoids 89–90
Hanover 51
Henry VIII 14
hepatitis 40
Herschel, William 43
Hesperus (ship) 114, 115, 118, 123
Hillary, Edmund 80
Hinduism 191–192
history
   complications and contradictions 198–199, 200
   debates and consensus 46–47, 54–55
history and context 13, 20
honour lists 137, 203
hotels 158–161
hunting 171, 203

I
Imperial hotel, Delhi 160
imperialism
   sport 59, 99
   values 59, 84, 99, 143
indentured labour 116–122
independence
   India 157, 170, 174, 184, 185, 188, 191, 192–194
   Nigeria 112
   USA 21, 190
India
   British Empire 99–100, 101, 151, 167–168
   caste system 191–192
   diaspora 123
   East India Company 160, 167, 171
   imperial hotels 159–160
   indentured labour 116, 118–119, 120, 122–123
   independence 157, 170, 174, 184, 185, 188, 191, 192–194
   looting 156
   Mughal emperors 168
   non-cooperation movement 185–186
   Partition 132, 192–193
   place names 43

   Salt March 183–184, 186–188, 191
   visit of George V and Mary 164–166, 168–174
Indian National Congress 185, 188, 190, 191
Indigenous Americans 23–24, 30, 33–34, 39
INGOs (international non-governmental organizations) 143–144
internet 124, 127–128
Iraq 137, 138–139
Ireland 4, 12, 13–15, 19, 23
Irish Sea 10–11
iron pyrite 30
Irwin, Lord 190
Israel 139
Italy 52
ivory 96, 203

J
Jakarta 73
Jamaica 6, 77, 122
James I 29, 37
Jamestown. 29–30, 35, 42

K
Kalahari Desert 83
kangaroos 72
Kew Gardens 74
Kidd, William, Captain 11
King, Martin Luther 191
Kipling, Rudyard 108
Kitchener, Lord 156
Koh-i-Noor diamond 95
Kolkata 43, 159–160

L
Lake Tanganyika 88
Lake Victoria 85, 92
language, English 22
Lawrence, T. E. 135
lions 81–82
Livingstone, David
   background 81
   death 89–90
   early adventures 81–83
   heart of Africa exploration 83, 84–85
   legacy 90
   marriage and family 83
   Nile source 85–89
   quotations 80, 83, 88, 89
London Vegetarian Society 185
London Zoo 173
looting 56, 95, 139, 153–156, 202

M

Mackinder, Halford 92
MacRobertson International Croquet Shield 59
malaria 73, 90
Māori peoples 71
Mary, Queen 164–165
Mauritius 122
Medina, RMS 164–165, 173
mercenaries 16
Middle East 132, 139
Middle Passage 47–50, 54
missionaries 80, 81, 83–84
Molehabangwe, Mebalwe 82
moon, surface area 2
Morris, Jan 6
Morse, Samuel 125
Mosi-oa-Tunya 84
Mount Everest 148
Mount Kenya 92
Mount Vesuvius 52
mountaineering 135, 148
Mughal emperors 168
Mumbai 43, 160
museums, returning loot 56, 155

N

Nasrullah Kahn, Emir of Bukhara 102–104, 106–108
national parks 144–145
Nehru, Jawaharlal 188
Nelson, Horatio 52
Nepal 171–173
New England 23–24
New Zealand 70–71, 123
Nigeria 6, 109–112
Nigerian Civil War 112
Nile source 80, 85–89, 92
non-cooperation movement 185–186
Normans 13

O

oil 138–139
O'Malley, Gráinne
 background 12–13, 15
 clan and children 16, 18, 19, 20
 imprisonment 18
 meets Elizabeth I 19
 pirate career 15–16
O'Malley, Owen 18
O'Malley, Tibbot 16, 18, 19
Ottoman Empire 134–135, 138
Oxford, University of 133–134

P

Pakistan 6, 112, 132, 192–193
Palestine 139
Partition 132, 192–193
Persia 100–101, 134
piles 89–90
Pilgrim Fathers 42
pirates
 compared to privateers 11–12
 Irish Sea 10–11
place names 30, 41–44, 71, 72, 84, 85, 203
planets 43, 63
plantations 50, 115, 116–118, 119–121
Pluto (planet) 2
Plymouth 41, 42
Pocahontas
 conversion and second marriage 35–36
 death 34, 38, 39
 Disney version 30–33, 34, 38
 first marriage 34
 names 32
 taken hostage 34–35
 travels to England 36–38
powder monkeys 50–51
Powhatan 30, 35
Prime Meridian 177–178
prisoner deportations 74
prisons 103–106
privateers 11–12
protectorates 110–112
Prussia 51
Puritans 22–24, 42

Q

questions, asking 202–203

R

racism 6, 38–39, 91, 160, 199
Raffles Hotel 158–159, 161
Raffles, Thomas Stamford 158–159
rail travel 176
Raleigh, Walter 28
religion in Britain 14–15, 22
reparation debates 202
repatriation 56
restitution 155
rhinos 173
Rhodes, Cecil 91–92
Richmond, Thomas 68
Ridgeway, Thomas 10
Rio de Janeiro 68
rivers, longest 85
Roanoke 28

Rolfe, John 35
Roman Empire 4
Royal African Company 94–95
royal family 93–96, 203
Royal Navy 50–51
Royal Niger Company 110
Royal Observatory 176–177
Royal Society 73–74
Rugby School 99
rum 120
Russia 2, 51, 98, 101, 151

S

salt 182–183
Salt March 183–184, 186–188, 191
Save the Children 142, 144
Saxony 51
schools
 Africa 111, 144
 on British Empire 5–6
Second World War 192
Seven Years War 51
Shepheard's Hotel, Cairo 160
ships
 crossing the line 69–70
 Equiano's narrative 50–52
 First Fleet 74
 Hesperus and *Whitby* 114, 115, 118, 123
 HMS *Bounty* 78
 HMS *Endeavour* 62, 66–73, 74–75, 76
 powder monkeys 50–51
 RMS *Medina* 164–165, 173
 slave trade 47–50
 travel risks 10–11
Sierra Leone 52, 112
Sikkim 151
Singapore 112, 158–159
slave trade *see also*
 abolitionist movement
 breadfruit 77–78
 British Empire 5
 Central Asia 101–102
 compared to indentured labour 121–122
 compensation payments to slave owners 117, 202
 dehumanization 53
 East Africa 82–84
 emancipation 116
 Equiano's narrative 50–51, 54–55, 203
 Middle Passage 47–50, 54
 purchasing freedom 51
 Royal African Company 94–95
 Sierra Leone colony 52
Slave Trade Act 116

smallpox 39, 40, 74
Smith, John 29, 30, 32, 33-34
Solander, Daniel 66, 68
Sons of Africa 52
South Africa 81, 91, 185
South Africa Company 91
South Pacific 62-64, 70
Spain 15, 28, 51
Speke, John Hanning 85, 92
spice trade 167
spies 102, 133, 137
spoils of war 154
Spöring, Herman 66
sport 57-59, 99
Sri Lanka 160
St Vincent 77
Star Wars 130
Stoddart, Charles 102-103, 104, 106
suffragettes 139-141
sugar 115, 116, 118, 119-120
sun, distance from Earth 63-64
sundials 175-176
Surville, Jean-François de 64
Sweden 51
Sykes-Picot Agreement 138-139

T
Tahiti 63, 70, 74, 75
Taj Mahal Palace, Mumbai 160
Te Kurī a Pāoa 71
tea 6, 188, 190
Tearfund 142
telegraphs 125
The Simpsons 32
Tibet 148-149, 151-156
Tierra del Fuego 68
tigers 172
TIME magazine 190
time zones 175-179
Tipu's Tiger 156
toads 65

Torres Strait Islander peoples 71, 72, 74, 75
trade *see also* slave trade
  Africa 90-91, 110
  East India Company 167
travel, time length of journeys 10, 100, 165
Treaty of Lhasa 152-153
Triangular Trade 48-50
Trinidad 122
tuberculosis 39
Tupaia 70
Turkey 135
Turkmenistan 101

U
untouchability 191-192
Uranus 43
USA
  culture from British Empire 21-22, 24-25
  independence 190
  Indigenous Americans 23-24, 30, 33-34, 39
  Irish immigration 24
  Massachusetts Bay colony 40, 42
  place names 41-42
  Puritans 22-24, 42
  Roanoke colony 28
  Virginia Company and Jamestown 29-30, 36
UTC (Coordinated Universal Time) 179
Uttamatomakkin 36
Uzbekistan 101

V
Vassa, Gustavus *see* Equiano, Olaudah
vegetarians 185
Venus 63-64, 70
viceroys 168, 190

Victoria 94, 96, 168
Victoria and Albert Museum (V&A) 156
Victoria Falls 84
Victoria (place name) 41
Virginia Company 29-30, 36
Virginia, USA 29-30, 34, 50
volcanos 52
voting rights 139-141

W
Waddell, Laurence 151, 154-155
Wakotani 83, 86
War of Independence, USA 21
wars, spoils of 154
Werowocomoco 30
West Indies 50
Whitby (ship) 114, 115, 118, 123
Whitehall Palace 94
William IV 96
William, Prince 96
Winthrop, John 40
Wolff, Joseph 106-107
women
  education 133-134
  right to vote 139-141
world records 148

Y
York 41
Young, Nicholas 68, 69, 70-71, 73
Younghusband, Expedition 148-155
Younghusband, Francis Edward 148, 149, 156-157

Z
Zambezi River 84-85
Zambia 91
Zanzibar 86
Zimbabwe 91, 112

ABOUT THE AUTHOR

Sathnam Sanghera was born to Punjabi immigrant parents in Wolverhampton in 1976. He entered the education system unable to speak English, but went on to graduate from Christ's College, Cambridge, with a first-class degree in English Language and Literature. He has been shortlisted for the Costa Book Awards twice, for his memoir *The Boy With the Topknot* and his novel *Marriage Material*. *Empireland* was a *Sunday Times* bestseller that was longlisted for the Baillie Gifford Prize for Non-Fiction, and won the Nibbies Book of the Year for Non-Fiction: Narrative in 2022. *Empireworld*, his ground-breaking follow-up to *Empireland*, was published in 2024 and was an instant *Sunday Times* bestseller. He lives in London.

ABOUT THE ILLUSTRATOR

Jen Khatun is a children's book illustrator of Bangladeshi/Indian heritage, who grew up in the beautiful, quaint city of Winchester. She has published work with Macmillan Children's Books, Oxford University Press, Walker Books and many more. Inspired by her natural surroundings, her favourite childhood stories and the hidden magical moments found in everyday life, Jen loves nothing better than to create colourful illustrations that dance with playfulness, hum with nostalgia and bring a sense of uplifting appreciation to life and family. She now lives quietly by the coast in East Sussex, and you will often find her walking on the South Downs or by the sea with her fiancé and their dog, Juno, exploring away on their new adventure!

PRAISE FOR *EMPIRELAND*

'The real remedy is education of the kind that Sanghera has embraced – accepting, not ignoring, the past'
Gerard deGroot, *The Times*

'*Empireland* takes a perfectly judged approach to its contentious but necessary subject'
Jonathan Coe

'I only wish this book had been around when I was at school'
Sadiq Khan, Mayor of London

'This remarkable book shines the brightest of lights into some of the darkest and most misunderstood corners of our shared history'
James O'Brien

'A fascinating reckoning with a history of empire'
***Guardian*, 'Best Politics Books of 2021'**

'A balanced and insightful study of the British Empire and contemporary attitudes towards it'
***The Times*, 'Best Paperbacks of 2021'**

'[*Empireland*] should be on the compulsory reading list of every secondary school in the country'
John Simpson

PRAISE FOR *EMPIREWORLD*

'A wonderful book'
Rory Stewart

'Nuanced and deeply researched'
Financial Times

'Not just a welcome corrective but a book for our times'
Peter Frankopan

'An absolute masterpiece'
James O'Brien

'Puts Sanghera in the firmament of great imperial historians'
Yasmin Alibhai-Brown, *i*

'Profoundly moving'
Elizabeth Day

'If you thought *Empireland* was beautifully written, this follow-up takes you even further – on an extraordinary, entertaining and eye-opening journey around the globe'
Sadiq Khan, Mayor of London

'Once again, Sathnam Sanghera has advanced the civil conversation we all need to have about empire and its legacies'
Jonathan Coe

'One of my favourite writers and *Empireworld* is a must-read if you want to understand the world'
Greg James, BBC Radio

'Another smart, compassionate and essential book about the legacy of empire and our braided histories'
Meera Syal

'His writing on empire and colonialism will change how you understand modern Britain'
Bella Mackie

PRAISE FOR *STOLEN HISTORY*

'Something that really comes across in the book is Sanghera's faith in young people . . . to form their own judgements about the British Empire'
The Bookseller

'Conversational . . . with humour that feels ideally pitched to the older children it is aimed at'
Financial Times

'*Stolen History* is the perfect book for every school. All our young people need to know the truth about the British Empire. This book is accessible, expertly written and hugely important'
Jasbinder Bilan, award-winning children's author

'Illuminating'
Nigella Lawson

'Accessible whilst imparting broad knowledge, appealingly pitched but deeply serious, this historically rigorous book is a must-read for any child who wants to know the basic facts of empire but also to gain an accurate sense of the wide variety of colonial activities which happened during four centuries of British colonial rule. *Stolen History* will inform a whole generation. Parents should read it too!'
Corinne Fowler, Professor of Colonialism and Heritage, University of Leicester

'*Stolen History* is a truly remarkable achievement: a historically accurate, diligently researched and nuanced account of the British Empire that is also gripping for younger readers. I know of no other writer who could have accomplished such a feat'
Professor Alan Lester FRHistS,
Professor of Historical Geography and
Professor of History, La Trobe University

'Sanghera brilliantly demonstrates that history doesn't have to be dumbed down to be made accessible, nor does it need to be sensationalized to seem relevant. Written with integrity and a deep commitment to reveal how the past has shaped our present, the book will make young readers engage with history as more than just entertainment and it will encourage them to ask new questions'
Kim A. Wagner, Professor of Global
and Imperial History, School of History
Queen Mary, University of London